Introductory

Milestones

Workbook
with Test Preparation

Australia • Brazil • Japan • Korea • Mexico • Singapore • Spain • United Kingdom • United States

Milestones Introductory Workbook with Test Preparation

Editorial Director: Joe Dougherty

Publisher: Sherrise Roehr

Managing Editor: Carmela Fazzino-Farah

Associate Development Editor: Stephen Greenfield

Technology Development Editor: Debie Mirtle

Executive Marketing Manager: Jim McDonough

Director of Product Marketing: Amy T. Mabley

Product Marketing Manager: Katie Kelley

Assistant Marketing Manager: Andrea Bobotas

Director of Content and Media Production: Michael Burggren

Production Assistant: Mark Rzeszutek

Manufacturing Manager: Marcia Locke

Development Editor: Arley Gray

Composition and Project Management: MPS Limited, A Macmillan Company

Interior Design: Rebecca Silber

Cover Design: Page 2, LLC

Cover Image: Visions of America/Joe Sohm/Getty

ISBN-13: 978-1-4240-3204-4

ISBN-10: 1-4240-3204-0

Heinle
20 Channel Center Street
Boston, MA 02210
USA

Cengage Learning is a leading provider of customized learning solutions with office locations around the globe, including Singapore, the United Kingdom, Australia, Mexico, Brazil, and Japan. Locate your local office at:
international.cengage.com/region

Cengage Learning products are represented in Canada by Nelson Education, Ltd.

Visit Heinle online at **elt.heinle.com**

Visit our corporate website at **www.cengage.com**

Printed in the United States of America
6 7 8 9 10 11 12 17 16 15 14 13

Contents

Assessment Practice

Strategies for Testing Success

Good readers will develop many different reading skills. To become a good reader, you will need to learn to read different kinds of texts. Many tests measure your reading skills. You will soon take one of these tests. The test will ask many questions, each with four possible answers. You must choose the correct one.

Here are some of the things you will be tested on:

- The meanings of words
- The main idea of a passage
- What happens in a story
- Why an author wrote a passage
- Comparing two or more things
- Cause and effect
- Using materials to find information

Getting Ready for Test Day

The following is a list of things that can help you get ready for a test.

- Read at least thirty minutes per day.
- Practice reading different kinds of materials (newspapers, magazines, novels, stories, poetry, etc.).
- Set a daily time for studying and doing your homework.
- Set up a place to do your homework every day. Make sure it is quiet and well lit.
- Practice answering each kind of question that will be on the test.
- Review simple test-taking hints.
- Practice timed tests.
- Get enough sleep the night before the test.
- Eat a good breakfast on the day of the test.

What to Expect During a Test

The ***Milestones*** program will help you acquire and master the skills you will need to succeed in English. It will aid your progress in the following four skills: listening, speaking, reading, and writing.

You are about to take an assessment practice test. The purpose of the test is to measure your achievement in constructing meaning from a wide variety of texts. This practice includes many different kinds of reading passages followed by specific questions about the passages.

Each reading passage will be different. Some types of passages include factual articles, fictional stories, and poems. Always read the passages carefully. You can go back to a passage if you are not sure about something.

After reading each passage, you will then answer questions about the passages. Read the questions carefully. They will ask about parts of the passages such as facts, plot, or language.

On the actual test, you may also be given a map, chart, or picture. For those, you will have to read the titles and labels to answer the questions.

Your teacher will give you sample directions and questions before the test begins. Ask about anything you do not understand. Once the test begins, you will not be able to ask questions.

The test questions all have multiple-choice answers. A multiple-choice test item may ask you to answer a specific question, or it may ask you to complete a sentence. There will be four possible answers. Only one of them is correct. Read all of the choices carefully and choose the answer you think is correct. Don't spend too much time on one question. It is important to answer all of the questions on the test.

How to Read Questions

The following is a sample passage. Read the passage and then read the questions below.

Every morning, Isabella and her mother walk together to school. Isabella's mother always smiles and says, "Isabella, be careful when you cross the street." Her smile is gentle like a flower.

1 **Read this sentence from the passage.**

Be careful when you cross the street.

What does careful mean in this sentence?

A cautious

B bored

C happy

D tired

2 **Which word best tells about Isabella's mother's attitude toward Isabella?**

A patient

B clever

C nervous

D understanding

You will be asked to use a number two pencil on the test. Be sure to mark the correct answer on the answer sheet. Make sure the number on the answer sheet matches the number of the question. It is easy to make a mistake. If you do, your answers will be marked as wrong because they are in the wrong place. Don't change an answer unless you are sure that it is wrong. If you must change an answer, check the number and change the right one. Make sure that you answer every question. Do not leave any answers blank.

How to Answer Questions

When answering multiple-choice questions, read each answer carefully.

3 **Read this sentence from the passage.**

Her smile is gentle like a flower.

What kind of sentence is this?

A simile

B metaphor

C onomatopoeia

D personification

If you come across an item that you do not know the answer to, here is one strategy you can use.

You might say: *There aren't any sounds in the sentence, so it is not onomatopoeia. There is no comparison to a person, so it is not personification. There is a comparison of one thing to another thing in this sentence, so it could be a metaphor. However, the word "like" is used, so it must be a simile. Therefore, the correct answer is letter a. This question is number 3. I will look at my answer sheet, find number 3, and mark letter a.*

The following pages contain a sample test. Read each passage carefully. Then use the answer sheet on page 5 to mark your answers.

Assessment Practice Test

Answer the questions that appear in the Assessment Practice Test on this Answer Sheet.

1 Ⓐ Ⓑ Ⓒ Ⓓ
2 Ⓐ Ⓑ Ⓒ Ⓓ
3 Ⓐ Ⓑ Ⓒ Ⓓ
4 Ⓐ Ⓑ Ⓒ Ⓓ
5 Ⓐ Ⓑ Ⓒ Ⓓ
6 Ⓐ Ⓑ Ⓒ Ⓓ
7 Ⓐ Ⓑ Ⓒ Ⓓ
8 Ⓐ Ⓑ Ⓒ Ⓓ
9 Ⓐ Ⓑ Ⓒ Ⓓ
10 Ⓐ Ⓑ Ⓒ Ⓓ
11 Ⓐ Ⓑ Ⓒ Ⓓ
12 Ⓐ Ⓑ Ⓒ Ⓓ
13 Ⓐ Ⓑ Ⓒ Ⓓ
14 Ⓐ Ⓑ Ⓒ Ⓓ
15 Ⓐ Ⓑ Ⓒ Ⓓ
16 Ⓐ Ⓑ Ⓒ Ⓓ
17 Ⓐ Ⓑ Ⓒ Ⓓ
18 Ⓐ Ⓑ Ⓒ Ⓓ
19 Ⓐ Ⓑ Ⓒ Ⓓ
20 Ⓐ Ⓑ Ⓒ Ⓓ
21 Ⓐ Ⓑ Ⓒ Ⓓ
22 Ⓐ Ⓑ Ⓒ Ⓓ
23 Ⓐ Ⓑ Ⓒ Ⓓ
24 Ⓐ Ⓑ Ⓒ Ⓓ
25 Ⓐ Ⓑ Ⓒ Ⓓ
26 Ⓐ Ⓑ Ⓒ Ⓓ
27 Ⓐ Ⓑ Ⓒ Ⓓ
28 Ⓐ Ⓑ Ⓒ Ⓓ
29 Ⓐ Ⓑ Ⓒ Ⓓ
30 Ⓐ Ⓑ Ⓒ Ⓓ
31 Ⓐ Ⓑ Ⓒ Ⓓ
32 Ⓐ Ⓑ Ⓒ Ⓓ
33 Ⓐ Ⓑ Ⓒ Ⓓ
34 Ⓐ Ⓑ Ⓒ Ⓓ
35 Ⓐ Ⓑ Ⓒ Ⓓ
36 Ⓐ Ⓑ Ⓒ Ⓓ
37 Ⓐ Ⓑ Ⓒ Ⓓ
38 Ⓐ Ⓑ Ⓒ Ⓓ
39 Ⓐ Ⓑ Ⓒ Ⓓ
40 Ⓐ Ⓑ Ⓒ Ⓓ
41 Ⓐ Ⓑ Ⓒ Ⓓ
42 Ⓐ Ⓑ Ⓒ Ⓓ
43 Ⓐ Ⓑ Ⓒ Ⓓ
44 Ⓐ Ⓑ Ⓒ Ⓓ
45 Ⓐ Ⓑ Ⓒ Ⓓ
46 Ⓐ Ⓑ Ⓒ Ⓓ
47 Ⓐ Ⓑ Ⓒ Ⓓ
48 Ⓐ Ⓑ Ⓒ Ⓓ
49 Ⓐ Ⓑ Ⓒ Ⓓ
50 Ⓐ Ⓑ Ⓒ Ⓓ
51 Ⓐ Ⓑ Ⓒ Ⓓ
52 Ⓐ Ⓑ Ⓒ Ⓓ
53 Ⓐ Ⓑ Ⓒ Ⓓ
54 Ⓐ Ⓑ Ⓒ Ⓓ
55 Ⓐ Ⓑ Ⓒ Ⓓ
56 Ⓐ Ⓑ Ⓒ Ⓓ
57 Ⓐ Ⓑ Ⓒ Ⓓ
58 Ⓐ Ⓑ Ⓒ Ⓓ
59 Ⓐ Ⓑ Ⓒ Ⓓ
60 Ⓐ Ⓑ Ⓒ Ⓓ
61 Ⓐ Ⓑ Ⓒ Ⓓ
62 Ⓐ Ⓑ Ⓒ Ⓓ
63 Ⓐ Ⓑ Ⓒ Ⓓ

The Little Shepherd

A Uyghur Folktale

1 Once there was a little shepherd named Aniz. He spent each day herding sheep. He was very gentle and kind. All of the sheep and people loved him. He had a bamboo flute that he liked to play.

2 Aniz worked for a mean boss who was always angry with him. "Do I pay you to sit around and play the flute?" he would ask.

3 Aniz was very good at being a shepherd. The sheep loved him and followed him happily. His flute never got in the way of his work.

4 One day the boss got very angry with Aniz for no reason. He broke his flute and shouted at him. Then he said he didn't want Aniz to work for him anymore.

5 An old man saw the boss yell at Aniz. "Don't worry Aniz," the old man said. "I'll help you make a new flute. Soon, you'll be happier than ever."

6 The old man was a master flute player. He helped Aniz carve a new flute. It was better and more beautiful in tone than his old flute. He also gave Aniz lessons to be a great flute player.

7 Now Aniz could play for all of his friends. Sometimes the animals of the forest would come and listen, too. Aniz became friends with the animals. He would go into the woods to play his flute for them. They loved to listen to him.

8 One night, the mean boss had a dream about an animal in the forest. He dreamed about a white rabbit with a black spot on its head. He woke up and told his sons about the dream. He said, "Whoever catches that rabbit will inherit my entire property."

9 The sons ran together to the forest to find the rabbit. They looked and looked, but found nothing.

10 Finally, the boss went into the forest himself. He came into the clearing where Aniz was playing his flute. Aniz was very angry when he saw him. He began to play his flute loudly. All of the animals surrounded the boss. Birds, bears, rabbits, wolves, snakes, and foxes all started walking closer to him.

11 "Do you remember me?" Aniz said. "If I play the flute now, these animals will eat you.

12 The mean boss was frightened. "Please have mercy," he said. "Do not treat me as I treated you. I'm so sorry. I'll give you anything if you spare my life."

13 Aniz said, "I'll let you live. But you must learn to be nice. You should not bully other people. Also, you must give half of your wealth to the poor people in the village. Do you understand?"

14 The boss agreed. He ran home to the village, crying all the way. He was never mean to anyone again. The animals of the forest and the villagers loved Aniz even more than before.

The Dragon and His Grandmother

1 Once, there lived three poor farmers. They worked hard to grow wheat during the hot summer days. The boss was mean and only paid them half of what he promised. One day, the men decided to run away. They hid in the field and waited. Soon it was night time. They stood up and got ready to leave.

2 Suddenly a dragon flew by. The dragon stopped and asked the men why they were hiding. They told the dragon how mean the boss was and that they wanted to go home. The dragon said, "I will bring you home. And I will give you this magic bell. If you ring it, you will be rich. But there is a cost. After seven years, I will come to you. You must guess my secret rhyme or serve me forever."

3 The men were afraid, but they needed the dragon's help. They accepted the offer. The dragon let them climb onto his back. Then he flew to their homes. The men were happy to see their families. They used the magic bell to buy new clothes, new houses, and everything anyone could want.

4 They lived rich and happy lives for seven years. Then, it was time for the dragon to return. They knew he would ask if they knew his secret rhyme, but they knew they could not guess it.

5 The day before the dragon came, the men met in a field. An old woman saw them together and asked, "Why are you so unhappy?" They told her the story and asked her opinion. She said, "Send the bravest of you into the woods. Look for help in the little house that looks like a pile of stones."

6 The bravest one went into the forest and found the little house. He went inside and found a very old woman who was the dragon's grandmother. He told her the story and asked for her help. The dragon's grandmother was a very nice lady. She told him to hide in the corner and she would get the rhyme.

7 That night, the dragon came to his grandmother for dinner. "I am going to collect three men tomorrow," he said. "They will never guess my secret rhyme." Then, he spoke his rhyme:

"I eat my porridge with raindrops
I've done it all my life.
I spread my bread with clouds,
and a sunbeam is my knife."

8 After eating dinner, the dragon left. Then, the man came out from the corner. He thanked the dragon's grandmother and went home.

9 The next day, the dragon found the men in the clearing. He was confident no one would guess his clever rhyme. "Have you guessed my rhyme?" he asked.

10 The men smiled and said the rhyme. The dragon was angry. He stomped on the ground, but he couldn't do anything. The men were free. They kept the magic bell and lived happily ever after.

1 **How did the new flute compare to the old flute in "The Little Shepherd"?**

A It was more colorful.

B It was larger.

C It sounded better.

D It was harder to play.

2 **What is the theme of the story?**

A Do not be mean to other people.

B Work hard for your money.

C Do not let play get in the way of work.

D Help people when they are sad.

3 **Read this sentence from paragraph 1.**

He spent each day herding sheep.

What is the meaning of spent in this sentence?

A paid

B wore out

C passed the time

D used up

4 **What kind of writing is this?**

A fiction

B play

C nonfiction

D poem

5 **Why did the author tell the story?**

A to give information

B to change your mind

C to teach a lesson

D to make you laugh

6 **What happened before the boss fired Aniz?**

A An old man made Aniz a flute.

B People felt sorry for Aniz.

C All of the animals surrounded the boss.

D Aniz worked as a shepherd.

7 **What kind of story is "The Dragon and His Grandmother"?**

A a play

B a poem

C historical fiction

D a fairy tale

8 **Why did the men want to escape?**

A They did not like to work.

B The boss was mean.

C The other workers were mean.

D They had to work over the weekend.

9 **What word best describes the dragon's grandmother?**

A mean

B selfish

C worried

D helpful

10 **What did the men need to know to be free?**

A a code

B a rhyme

C a password

D a hiding place

11 **Which word is related to the word escape?**

A memory

B magic

C freedom

D warning

12 **What is true about both of these passages?**

A They are true stories.

B They give us information.

C They are made-up stories.

D They are about real people.

The May Queen's Ball

1 Stella lived in a small cottage on the edge of the woods. She loved to gather flowers from the fields. She found the prettiest flowers to bring home. One day, she woke up to find that yesterday's flowers had already wilted. They had been pretty pink tulips and blue hyacinths.

2 Her father saw her frowning into the flowers. "Why are you so sad, little one?" he asked.

3 "The flowers look tired," she said, "and I just picked them yesterday."

4 "Oh, but they have been on an adventure," he said. "Haven't you heard of the May Queen's ball? It happens every spring. The May Queen holds a party in the center of the forest. It's always in a secret place. All of the flowers want to go. They save up their color to look best for the ball. Then they spend all night dancing. By the end of the night, they are tired. I'm surprised your flowers made it home."

5 "Who is this May Queen?" asked Stella. "Why does she want my flowers?"

6 "The May Queen is a beautiful white flower that blooms in the middle of the forest. She is the queen of the spring flowers. She invites all of the flowers to her ball. And all of the flowers want to go."

7 Stella was quiet for a moment. This ball sounded wonderful. All of the flowers in their brightest colors, dancing together with the mysterious May Queen.

8 "How can I see the May Queen's ball?" she asked. "I'd like to see the flowers dancing together. I want to see the May Queen."

9 Her father smiled. "The party is not for people. It's for flowers. The May Queen doesn't like being seen. You have to follow the flowers. But it won't happen again until next year."

10 Stella waited. She waited through spring. She waited through summer. She waited through fall. When winter came, she started to think of the beautiful flowers.

11 Soon spring came. The weather got warmer. The flowers started to bloom. Each day, she thought about the May Queen.

12 Then, one day, she fell asleep in the garden under the afternoon sun. She woke to soft whispers. When she opened her eyes, she saw one flower talking to another.

13 Stella pretended to be asleep but kept her eyes open a little. She saw the flowers change into butterflies. The butterflies flew toward the forest. They flew quickly, but Stella ran after them.

14 Finally they reached the center of the forest. Stella saw a field of flowers dancing under the sun. In the center of the flowers there was a chair made of green leaves. On the chair sat a brilliant white flower. It was the May Queen.

The Day Pirates Took Over the School

1 It happened during lunch. A man dressed in colorful clothing walked into the cafeteria. He had one healthy leg and one wooden leg. He also had a parrot on his shoulder. He was a pirate captain!

2 Several other pirates were also standing with him. They wore bandanas on their heads and striped socks on their feet. They had large shoes and short pants. They stayed by the door, but the captain walked forward.

3 Everybody stopped eating as the pirate captain walked into the center of the room. Two fourth graders helped him climb on top of a table. It's hard to climb with a wooden leg. The captain brushed off his coat and stood up straight. "Ahoy mateys!" he yelled.

4 "Ahoy!" yelled everyone in the lunchroom. Mr. Schneckenfuss, my teacher, did not seem happy about the captain standing on a table. The pirates smiled at him. One of them had a monkey.

5 "I'm Captain Blue Bart and this is my crew," the captain said. He pointed to the group of men in the corner. The pirates waved.

6 "We've come to ask you a question. We'd like to know if you want to see our pirate ship," the captain said.

7 The students cheered, whistled, and clapped. The fourth graders helped the captain down from the table, and everyone followed them out of the lunchroom: pirates, children, a monkey, and a parrot.

8 Captain Blue Bart, Melon Wallace, Jim Jumblebee, and all of the pirates took us around their ship. Some older kids were allowed to climb the ropes. They showed us how the cannons worked and even let us taste their food.

9 But soon it was time for them to leave. We asked if we could stay, but the captain said they had to sail on. Our parents wouldn't want us to leave with them. The pirates were sorry to see us go, too. They waved and some of them even cried into their bandanas.

10 I heard the parrot squawk, "Good-bye! Good-bye!" Then, I ran to catch the bus home. I tried to look from the bus window, but the ship was gone.

11 The next day everything was back to normal at school. I almost thought it was a dream. Then I saw Mr. Schneckenfuss walking down the hallway. As he passed me, I heard him say, "Ahoy!"

13 **What kind of writing is the passage, "The May Queen's Ball"?**

A poem

B fantasy

C play

D nonfiction

14 **Which word best describes Stella?**

A curious

B sad

C angry

D tired

15 **What did the flowers change into?**

A birds

B bees

C butterflies

D bunnies

16 **How did Stella know it was time for the ball?**

A It was summer.

B It was spring.

C It was fall.

D It was winter.

17 **Read this sentence from paragraph 1.**

> She loved to gather flowers from the fields.

What is the meaning of gather in this sentence?

A plant

B pick

C watch

D grow

18 **Why is Stella sad when the story begins?**

A She could not go to the ball.

B She was lost in the woods.

C Her flowers were dying.

D She is all by herself.

19 **What kind of writing is the passage, "The Day Pirates Took Over the School"?**

A poetry

B drama

C fiction

D nonfiction

20 **How did the children feel when the pirates asked them to see their ship?**

A scared

B excited

C sad

D disappointed

21 **Why did the captain need help to get on the table?**

A It was too high.

B He had a patch on his eye.

C There was food all over.

D He had a wooden leg.

22 **Where did the story take place?**

A at school

B at the movies

C near the ocean

D in a parking lot

Nana's Store

1 My Nana always says you have to take care of your neighbors. She should know. She sees most of the neighborhood every day.

2 Nana runs a corner grocery store on a busy city street. Her store carries everything people need: soap, batteries, chickens, and card tables. She also sells fresh fruit and vegetables.

3 Nana always knows what's happening in the neighborhood. Everyone brings news to the store. "It's small," she says, "but the whole world comes in through my door."

4 She knows who's sick, who has a new baby, and who's getting married. A lot of people come to the store just to talk. In the summer, Nana puts chairs outside so they can sit under the awning. In the winter, they drink coffee and lean against the refrigerator.

5 My whole family works at the store. Uncle Louie and Aunt Mimi help when the big vegetable trucks come. My Nana can't lift the fruit boxes as easily as they can. My cousins also work at the store. My mother grew up working with Nana. She says that's why she's good at math. She's an accountant now.

6 The big supermarkets make more money than Nana's store. Their prices are very low. Sometimes if the supermarket has a sale, Nana tells people to go there instead. They buy a lot of goods if they are cheap. Then Nana sells them at our store for the same price.

7 Nana always helps people. Sometimes people don't have enough money to pay for their food. Nana records everything carefully. She always gives people food when they need it. They always pay her back.

8 In all the time Nana has owned the store, she has never had any big problems. No one has ever tried to break into Nana's store and steal things. This has happened to other business owners but not to her.

9 Nana says it's because she takes care of her neighbors.

23 **What is the theme of the the passage "Nana's Store"?**

A Be kind and others will be kind to you.

B Only worry about yourself.

C Never trust anyone but family.

D Don't bother with your neighbors.

24 **Which character in the story is an accountant now?**

A Uncle Louie

B the narrator

C the narrator's mother

D Nana

25 **How would the people feel if Nana's store closed?**

A worried

B upset

C happy

D lonely

26 **Read this sentence from paragraph 8.**

> No one has ever tried to <u>break</u> into Nana's store and steal things.

What is the meaning of <u>break</u> in this sentence?

A to fall apart

B to make known

C to force a way into

D to become fair

27 **What word best describes Nana?**

A mean

B caring

C worthless

D curious

The Tree Cycle

In summer when the world is hot
the summer leaves are cool and green.
The world is shady underneath
the wealth of summer trees.

In autumn when the cold wind comes 5
the trees turn red and rust and gold.
Their colors fall to earth and roam
in heaps of autumn flames.

In winter when the ice is thick
the trees stand patiently by. 10
Their branches stretch as bare as sticks
across the winter sky.

In spring the new leaves come again
as suddenly as a surprise.
They open to the waiting world 15
new faces to new light.

The trees reflect the passing time
in costumes wild and weird.
They cycle through the changing world,
all colors of the year. 20

Shade they give, then take away
but not before fall's bright display.
We see them in so many ways
and trees always amaze.

28 **What kind of writing is "The Tree Cycle"?**

A drama

B poetry

C fiction

D nonfiction

29 **Read these lines from the poem.**

> The world is shady underneath
> the wealth of summer trees.

What is the meaning of the words wealth of summer trees?

A money

B leaves

C fruit

D branches

30 **What does the author compare the trees' autumn colors to?**

A crayons

B birds

C flames

D flowers

31 **Read these lines from the poem.**

> Their colors fall to earth and
> roam in heaps of autumn
> flames.

What kind of phrase is in heaps of autumn flames?

A personification

B metaphor

C simile

D symbolism

32 **Read these lines from the poem.**

> In spring the new leaves
> come again as suddenly
> as a surprise.

What is as suddenly as a surprise?

A a rhyme

B alliteration

C onomatopoeia

D a word family

33 **What is a *synonym* for stretch? (stanza 3)**

A reach

B pull

C leap

D stray

How to Make a Marble Path

Here's a fun project for a rainy day. Build a path for marbles to roll down

You will need:

A large cardboard box
Cardboard tubes
Tape and scissors
Marbles
A clock with a second hand

Directions

1. Set up the large cardboard box as your base.
2. Tape the tubes to the box. You can wrap the tubes outside of the box or have them go through the inside.
3. Test your marble path. Use a clock to measure the time it takes for a marble to roll through.

How to Make a Peanut Butter Pinecone

Peanut Butter Pinecones are fun to make. Hang them outside for birds to enjoy.

You will need:

Large pinecones
Creamy peanut butter
Birdseed
A bowl
A spoon
A piece of string
Newspaper

Directions

1. Lay down newspaper to work on.
2. Pour the birdseed into a bowl.
3. Tie a piece of string to the pinecone.
4. Cover the pinecone with peanut butter with a spoon.
5. Roll the peanut butter pinecone in birdseed.
6. Put the pinecone on the newspaper to keep the table clean.
7. Hang the pinecone outdoors in a place that birds will like. Soon, they will come to the pinecone to eat the peanut butter.

34 **Why did the author write these passages?**

- **A** to explain a process
- **B** to tell a story
- **C** to make the reader laugh
- **D** to answer a question

35 **What is the first thing you must do for the marble path?**

- **A** Tape the tubes.
- **B** Test the path.
- **C** Make a base.
- **D** Time the marble.

36 **What helps the birdseed stick to the pinecone?**

- **A** pipe cleaners
- **B** the spoon
- **C** peanut butter
- **D** newspaper

37 **Why do you need newspaper?**

- **A** to read the directions
- **B** to keep the table clean
- **C** to wrap the pinecone
- **D** to learn about birds

38 **What is the last thing you do with the pinecone?**

- **A** Hang the pinecone outdoors.
- **B** Roll the pinecone in birdseed.
- **C** Cover the pinecone with peanut butter.
- **D** Make a loop with a pipe cleaner.

39 **What do these passages do?**

- **A** They give directions.
- **B** They tell a story.
- **C** They make us laugh.
- **D** They try to change our minds.

Meerkats

1 Meerkats are small animals related to the mongoose. They live in the Kalahari Desert in southern Africa. Meerkats have a range of fur colors. Their fur can be gray, orange, or brown. These colors match the colors of the desert.

2 Adult meerkats weigh about 2 pounds. They are usually 12 inches high standing up and 6 inches high with all four paws on the ground. Their tails are 8 inches long. This long tail helps meerkats stand up. They use their tail for balance when they stand.

3 Meerkats have interesting markings on their bodies. They have dark rings around their eyes and black tips on their tails. The dark rings help the meerkats see in sunny conditions. The black tips help meerkats find each other when they hunt together. Every meerkat has a different pattern on its back. Like snowflakes, no two are alike.

4 Meerkats live in large groups. Each group has 5 to 40 meerkats. They all sleep in the same burrow, hunt together, and take care of each other.

5 Meerkat burrows are systems of tunnels and rooms dug into the sand. They include sleeping rooms and many exits. They share their burrows with other animals like the yellow mongoose and ground squirrel.

6 Meerkats are very good at digging in the sand. They change their burrows often, so they have to dig new ones. They also dig in the sand for food. They have four claws on their paws for quick digging. They can also close their ears when they dig, which keeps them from getting sand in their ears.

7 Meerkats spend all day hunting for food. They go out and hunt together in groups. Some of the meerkats stand up and watch for danger. They are called "sentries." If they have young meerkats in the group, some stay behind as babysitters.

8 Meerkats eat many different things. They eat lizards, ant eggs, insects, worms, birds, small animals, and some roots. They even like eating scorpions! Meerkats are immune to many types of poison, so poisonous insects do not bother them.

9 Meerkats work hard to survive in the harsh desert conditions. They spend most of the time looking for food. They also have to watch out for predators: animals that hunt them. Meerkat predators are mainly eagles and jackals, as well as cobras and hyenas.

10 When a meerkat sentry sees a predator, he or she warns the group. All of the meerkats run and hide. They even build special holes to hide in called "bolt holes."

11 Warnings are only some of the sounds meerkats make. Meerkats talk to each other a lot. They can make over 20 different sounds with different meanings.

12 It's hard for a small animal to be alone in the desert. As a group, Meerkats take care of each other and help each other survive. But they are not all business. They also love to play when they are finished hunting.

40 **What is the meaning of <u>sentries</u> in paragraph 7 of the passage, "Meerkats"?**

A hunters

B families

C enemies

D guards

41 **What animals are friendly to meerkats?**

A cobras

B squirrels

C hyenas

D jackals

42 **What is the passage mostly about?**

A who the meerkats enemies are

B what meerkats look like

C how meerkats survive in the desert

D how meerkats find their food

43 **What is true about meerkats?**

A They take care of each other.

B They cannot eat poisonous insects.

C They stay in one burrow forever.

D They live alone in their own burrows.

44 **How do meerkats use their tails?**

A to warn of danger

B to keep their balance

C to dig their burrows

D to care for their babies

45 **What is a *synonym* for <u>mainly</u> (paragraph 9)?**

A hardly

B already

C mostly

D exactly

Meteors

Have you ever seen a shooting star? Shooting stars travel across the sky with a bright trail. You can see the trails for several minutes. Another name for shooting stars is meteors.

Meteors are pieces of dust from space. They enter the Earth's atmosphere. They leave a glowing trail because they move very quickly. Meteors travel 35 to 45 miles in one second.

Most meteors are small. They are the size of a grain of sand. There are also large meteors. Very large meteors are called "fireballs." Fireballs are heavy. The glowing tails on fireballs last a long time. Sometimes they explode and make a loud noise!

Most meteors burn up in the fall. However, some meteors can fall to Earth. Then they are called meteorites. Only a few larger meteorites fall to Earth every year. They are usually very small. A large meteorite is the size of a marble.

You can see meteors anywhere in the world. You don't need a telescope to see them. You just need a lot of patience. You can see a few meteors every hour in the night sky.

Sometimes there are big groups of meteors. These groups are called "meteor showers." There can be thousands of meteors in a meteor shower. Meteor showers are easy to find because they happen every year at the same time.

Science Textbook Index

S
safety 21, 57, 121–123
salt 76–86
salt water 80, 82–83
sand 34–38
    dollar 35
    stone 37
Saturn, rings of 84–85
    moons of 86
    See also Solar System
sea, salt 40–48
    level 40–42
    star 44

46 **What are meteors?**

A grains of sand

B pieces of dust

C small planets

D streams of sunlight

47 **Why do meteors have glowing trails?**

A They are so small.

B They explode in the sky.

C They last a long time.

D They travel very quickly.

48 **On what page can you find facts about sea stars?**

A 44

B 36

C 71

D 86

49 **Where can you find more facts about Saturn?**

A under sea salt

B under Solar System

C on page 21

D on pages 65–66

50 **What can you find out in an index?**

A where to find information

B facts about different animals

C the order that facts are given

D the author of the book

51 **What is true about both passages?**

A They tell a funny story.

B They give us directions.

C They give information.

D They try to change our minds.

Dr. Wah Hing, the Chinese Herb Doctor of Sacramento

1 "Dr. Yee, it's your turn!"

2 Yee Fung Cheung looked at the ivory pieces in front of him. He drew a piece. He thought about his next move.

3 Dr. Yee was playing mahjong with friends at the grocery store in the Chinese neighborhood of Sacramento. Dr. Yee came to California from China. He enjoyed playing the game to meet new friends and to see neighbors.

4 Dr. Yee put down a colorful spring tile. Suddenly, a man burst into the store. He was out of breath from running. He said, "Where's the doctor?"

5 Dr. Yee looked at him.

6 "I need a doctor immediately," the man said. "I stopped at the herb store. There was no one there."

7 Dr. Yee stood up. "I am the doctor," he said.

8 The man said, "I'm the cook for Governor Stanford. Mrs. Stanford is ill. The other doctors cannot help her."

9 Everyone in the grocery store was amazed. It was unusual in the 1860s for non-Chinese people to use Chinese medicines. The wife of the governor of California was not a common patient for a Chinese herbal doctor.

10 Dr. Yee thought only about the sick woman. "Come with me," he said.

11 The two men ran to the herb shop. On the way, Dr. Yee asked the cook about Mrs. Stanford's illness. Dr. Yee's father was also a doctor. He taught Dr. Yee to understand illnesses and to make medicine for them.

12 At the store, Dr. Yee put together several herbs to make Mrs. Stanford's prescription. She was having lung trouble. He made his best medicine for weak lungs.

13 The cook brought the medicine to the house. They gave it to Mrs. Stanford. She made a miraculous recovery. Everyone knew that Dr. Yee's herbal medicine was the cure.

14 The governor asked for the name of the doctor who saved his wife. The cook didn't remember. He was so worried about Mrs. Stanford, he forgot to ask. So he called Dr. Yee, "Dr. Wah Hing," which was the name of the grocery store.

15 Dr. Yee Fung Cheung saved the life of Mrs. Stanford in 1862. He became famous as Dr. Wah Hing. Today, his family still practices medicine in the Sacramento area. Dr. Yee's first herb shop, the Chew Kee Store in Fiddletown, California, is now a museum on the National Register of Historic Places.

Langston Hughes

Langston Hughes is a famous African-American poet and author. He was born in Missouri in 1902. His family didn't have much money.

Hughes wrote poems in high school. His first poem appeared in a magazine when he was 19. The magazine was called *The Crisis*. It was the magazine of the National Association for the Advancement of Colored People. This was a new group at the time.

Hughes moved to New York City to attend Columbia University. He studied engineering. He was a good student, but he left school without a degree. He wanted to be a writer.

In the 1920s, there were a lot of African-American artists in New York. They called this time the Harlem Renaissance. Harlem is a neighborhood in New York City. A lot of African-American artists lived there.

Hughes became a famous poet. He listened to jazz and blues music. He used them in his poetry. Poetry and music were important parts of the Harlem Renaissance.

Japanese Tea Ceremony

In Japan there is a special way of serving tea. It is called Japanese Tea Ceremony. This way of preparing and serving tea takes many years to learn. Only masters of Tea Ceremony can teach it. There are many things to learn about the tea. First, there are the kinds of tea. There is a thick tea and a thin tea. Both are made with green tea powder. Then there are special tools to make the tea. It takes a long time to learn how to use them. There are also special tools for serving tea to guests and special foods to make for them. The guests are very important. Everything has to be done properly for them. A full Japanese Tea Ceremony can take four hours! In this time, the guests drink the tea and enjoy the beauty of nature. Japanese Tea Ceremony is truly an art.

A History of Navajo Weaving

1 Weaving means making cloth from yarn or thread. The Navajo people of the American Southwest tell a story of how they learned to weave. They say Spider Woman showed them to weave with a tool called a loom. She made her loom out of the sky and the Earth. She made cloth out of sunlight, lightning, shells, and rock crystal.

2 Historians tell a different story. In the 1600s, the Navajo people met another group of people called the Pueblo. The Pueblo taught the Navajo to take wool from sheep and to weave it with looms.

3 Each year, sheep are shaved of their wool. The wool is cleaned and dyed. The Navajo often use dye made from vegetables. The wool is then dried. Then it is spun into yarn for weaving. The yarn is woven together on a loom to form woolen cloth.

4 Soon after the Navajo met the Pueblo, another group of people came to the land. They were from Spain, and they brought their own sheep and looms. The Navajo learned more about weaving from the Spanish. Their skill at weaving was very high.

5 The Navajo people became famous for their colorful blankets. European and Mexican traders paid a lot of money for Navajo blankets. They were warm and light and kept the water out like a raincoat. The Navajo also wove rugs, dresses, shirts, and other clothes.

6 In the 1800s, the U.S. government took the land from the Navajo people. Many Navajo people died. The others moved off the land. Many of their sheep were gone, so they could not weave as much.

7 Later, the Navajo returned to their land, where many still live today. Some traders started to move near the Navajo. They opened stores to buy and sell goods with the Navajo people. These traders asked the Navajo weavers to make special patterns and colors.

8 Today, most rugs and blankets are made in factories. However, Navajo rugs and blankets are still made by hand. It takes a weaver about 140 hours to weave a large blanket and 238 hours to weave a rug. Many people think they are works of art.

52 **In the story, "Dr. Wah Hing, the Chinese Herb Doctor of Sacramento," which word best describes Dr. Yee?**

A gentle

B clever

C helpful

D angry

53 **Who was ill?**

A the governor

B the governor's wife

C the governor's cook

D the governor's child

54 **Why did the cook call him Dr. Wah Hing?**

A He forgot the doctor's real name.

B The doctor told him to.

C That's what his friends called him.

D Wah Hing was the name of the medicine.

55 **Why did Langston Hughes leave Columbia University?**

A He wanted to be a writer.

B He was not doing well in school.

C He got a job as an engineer.

D He wanted to move to Harlem.

56 **Why would someone want to read Langston Hughes' poetry?**

A to learn about growing up in Kansas

B to learn about African-American culture

C to learn about different kinds of music

D to learn about the beauty of nature

57 **What do the passages "Dr. Wah Hing, the Chinese Herb Doctor of Sacramento" and "Langston Hughes" have in common?**

A both are about life in a big city

B both are about where to look for help

C both are about being an artist

D both are about real people

58 **Who performs at tea ceremonies?**

A anyone who wants to perform

B visitors from around the world

C people who have learned from masters

D sellers of powdered green tea

59 **What is the passage, "Japanese Tea Ceremony" mostly about?**

A different kinds of tea

B Japanese clothing

C school in Japan

D a special ceremony

60 **What is the meaning of colorful?**

A having many colors

B using only one color

C putting colors together

D adding colors to wool

61 **What did the traders do when the Navajo returned to their land?**

A They took the land from the Navajo people.

B They learned to weave from the Navajo.

C They started factories to make rugs.

D They opened stores to buy and sell goods.

62 **Why did the authors write these passages?**

A to give information

B to teach a lesson

C to make the reader laugh

D to try to change our minds

63 **What are both of these passages about?**

A skills that are important to different cultures

B things that are make-believe

C how to learn about history

D things that no longer exist

Name ______________________ Date ______________

Shape Recognition

A. Circle the same shapes.

Example: I	(I)	H	T	(I)	L	H	T	(I)	L	Z
1. **B**	P	R	B	ꓭ	B	ᗺ	D	ꟼ	B	3
2. **M**	Σ	W	V	M	N	Ƹ	M	ꟽ	M	Z
3. **S**	S	ᔕ	Ɔ	S	Z	C	S	ᔕ	S	Ɔ
4. **C**	G	C	O	Q	Ɔ	O	C	C	Ɔ	ᔕ
5. **N**	M	W	Z	N	Σ	V	M	N	И	N
6. **E**	F	E	Ǝ	⅃	W	E	Ǝ	Ⅎ	E	F
7. **L**	L	F	I	⅂	T	L	Ǝ	ꟻ	L	L
8. **O**	O	Q	C	Ɔ	O	⅁	O	Q	P	O
9. **Z**	Ƨ	N	W	Z	M	Z	ꟻ	Z	Γ	Z
10. **Q**	C	Ó	Q	Ɔ	O	Q	G	Q	Ϙ	D

B. Copy the pattern.

Example: / / \ \ | | ____ / / \ \ | | ____

1. \ \ | | / / ______________
2. < | | > | + ______________
3. + + + / / X ______________
4. — | — | — | ______________
5. O — O — | | ______________
6. — | X | — | ______________
7. (O) (X) ______________
8. | — / \ — | ______________
9. | | + + = = ______________
10. = | X | X + ______________

Name ______________________ Date ______________

Pre-Literacy

Trace over the lines.

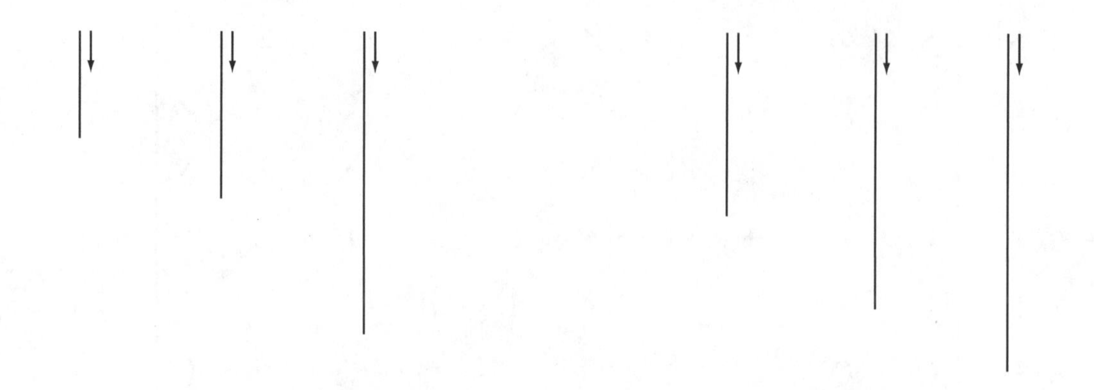

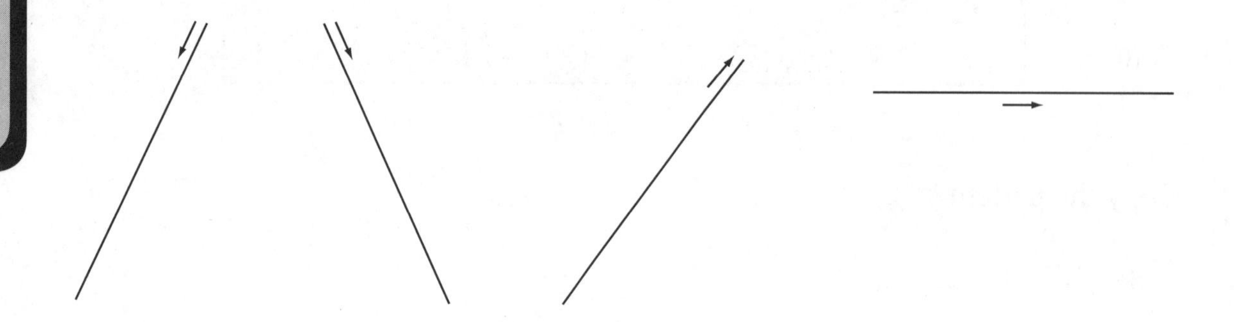

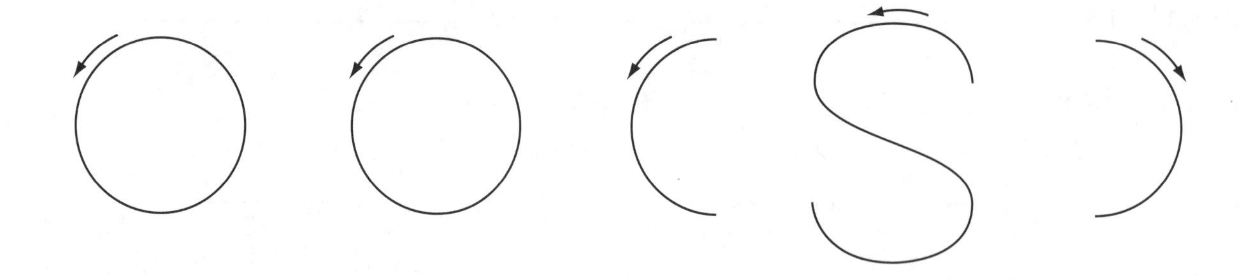

Name ______________________ Date ______________

Vocabulary

School

Use with student book pages 4–5.

A. Write the correct word from the box to go with each picture.

classmates	flag	map	nurse	principal	~~student~~	teacher

Example:  student

1.  ______________

2. ______________

3.  ______________

4.   ______________

5.  ______________

6.  ______________

B. Draw a picture of your school. Use all seven of the vocabulary words. Write the name of each vocabulary word that you use.

My School

Name ______________________ Date ______________

Listening and Speaking

Greetings and Introductions

Use with student book pages 6–7.

A. Match the two parts of the conversation.

Example: Hi, Pam. — e. Hello, Ms. Garcia.

1. Hi. My name is Sara Jones. What's your name?
2. I'm your teacher. My name is Mr. Allen.
3. Hello, Ms. Garcia. My name is Jade Lee.
4. Bye.

a. Good morning, Mr. Allen.
b. See you later.
c. Nice to meet you, Jade.
d. My name is Pedro Bautista.
e. Hello, Ms. Garcia.

B. Circle the correct way to write each person's name.

Example: (Mr. Bautista) Miss Bautista

1. Ms. Allen Mr. Allen

3. Miss Lee Mr. Lee

2. Mr. Garcia Ms. Garcia

C. Circle the greeting for each time of day.

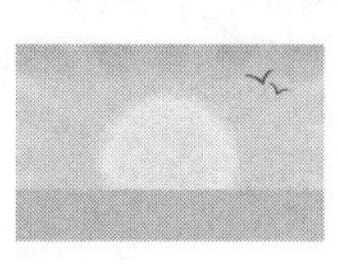

Example: (Good morning.) Good afternoon. Good evening.

1. Good morning. Good afternoon. Good evening.

2. Good morning. Good afternoon. Good evening.

Name ______________________ Date ______________

D. Write the word from the box to finish each sentence.

Example: Hi, Pam. Hello, Ms. Garcia.

Bye	~~Hello~~	Hi	later	meet	name	principal	teacher

1. ______________. My name is Sara Jones. What's your name?
2. My ______________ is Pedro Bautista.
3. Good morning. I'm your ______________. My name is Mr. Allen.
4. This is your ______________. Her name is Ms. Garcia.
5. Nice to ______________ you, Jade.
6. See you ______________.

E. Write the correct response.

~~My name is Ana.~~	Nice to meet you, too.	See you later.	Hello.

Example: What's your name? My name is Ana.

1. Hi. ______________
2. Nice to meet you. ______________
3. Bye. ______________

Name ______________________ Date ______________

Listening and Speaking

Saying Where You Are From

Use with student book pages 8–9.

A. Read the words. Circle the country's name.

Example: Afghan (Afghanistan)

1. American United States of America
2. Mexican Mexico
3. Brazilian Brazil
4. Haiti Haitian
5. Cambodian Cambodia
6. Somalia Somalian
7. Russian Russia
8. Chinese China
9. Cuban Cuba
10. Vietnam Vietnamese
11. Guatemala Guatemalan
12. Afghan Afghanistan

B. Write the word for each nationality.

Example: United States of America American

1. Vietnam ______________
2. Guatemala ______________
3. Cuba ______________
4. China ______________
5. Russia ______________
6. Cambodia ______________
7. Brazil ______________
8. Mexico ______________
9. Haiti ______________
10. Afghanistan ______________
11. Somalia ______________

Name ______________________ Date ______________

C. Write the name of the country to finish the sentence.

Example: He's Brazilian. He's from Brazil.

1. He's Afghani. He's from ______________.
2. She's Haitian. She's from ______________.
3. I'm Cuban. I'm from ______________.
4. They're Somalian. They're from ______________.
5. He's Cambodian. He's from ______________.
6. She's American. She's from the ______________.
7. I'm Mexican. I'm from ______________.
8. They're Brazilian. They're from ______________.

D. Draw and color the flag for each country.

China	Russia	Haiti
Somalia	Vietnam	Cuba

Name ______________________ Date ______________

Letters and Sounds

Use with student book pages 10–11.

Initial Consonants: b, c, f, g
Final Consonants: b, f, g

A. Say the word for the picture. Write the beginning letter.

Example:  b

1.  ____
4.  ____
6.  ____
2.  ____
5.  ____
7.  ____
3.  ____

B. Say the word for the picture. Write the last letter.

Example:  ca b

1. 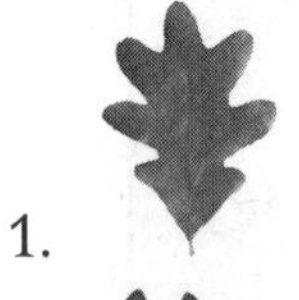 lea ___
3.  tu ___
5.  ca ___
2. do ___
4. 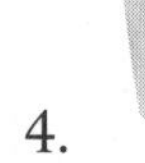 ba ___
6.  shel ___

C. Say the words. Then circle the two pictures that begin with the same sound.

Example: 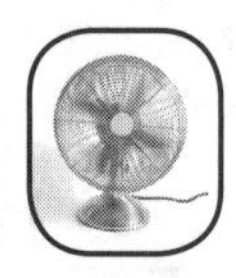 

1.   
3.   
2.    
4.   

Name ______________________________ Date ______________

Letters and Sounds

Use with student book pages 12–13.

Initial Consonants: m, p, s, t
Final Consonants: m, p, s, t

A. Circle the pictures for the two words that end with the same sound.

Example: 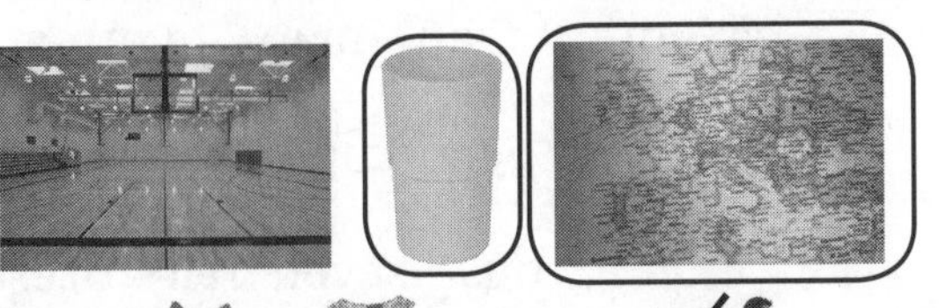

1. 

3. 

2. 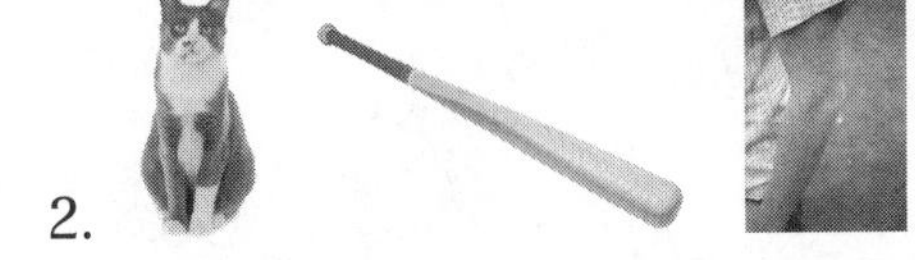

B. Look at the pictures. Write the missing letter.

Example:  b oy

 ca b

1.  ____ an

 ar ____

2.  ____ even

 bu ____

3.  ____ encil

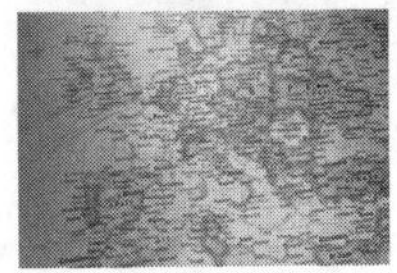 ma ____

C. Write the word for each picture in the crossword puzzle.

Example: a.  b. 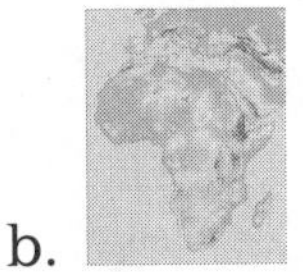

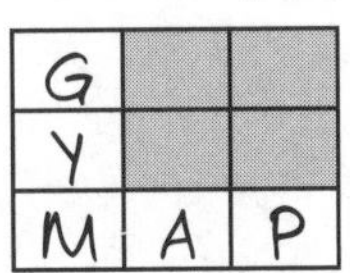

1. a. 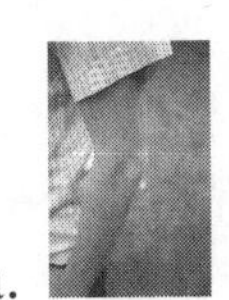 b. 

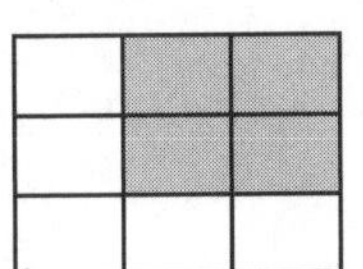

2. a. b. 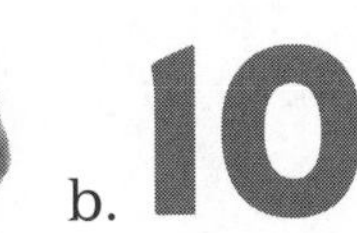

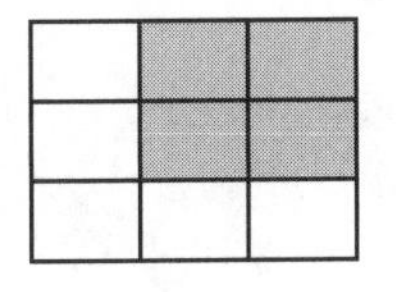

Name ______________________ Date ______________

Writing the Alphabet

Use with student book page 14.

A. Say the name of the letter. Read each word. Circle that letter in each word.

Example: b (b)oy (b)ook tu(b)

1. **c** car cab cup cat
2. **f** fan leaf five shelf
3. **g** girl bag dog good-bye
4. **b** book cab tub boy
5. **m** man map gym arm
6. **p** pen cup map pencil
7. **s** bus seven sit dress
8. **t** cat ten bat teacher

B. Match the capital and lowercase letters.

Example: Q	d
1. D	n
2. Z	q
3. B	r
4. N	b
5. R	z

C. Write the matching capital or lowercase letter.

Example: A ___a___

1. C ____
2. v ____
3. H ____
4. l ____
5. U ____
6. w ____
7. G ____
8. k ____
9. M ____
10. f ____
11. J ____
12. k ____

Name ______________________ Date ______________

Writing the Alphabet

Use with student book page 15.

A. Write the capital and lowercase letters.

Example: A a 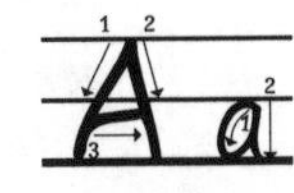

1. A a ________
2. B b ________
3. C c ________
4. D d ________
5. E e ________
6. F f ________
7. G g ________
8. H h ________
9. I i ________
10. J j ________
11. K k ________
12. L l ________
13. M m ________
14. N n ________
15. O o ________
16. P p ________
17. Q q ________
18. R r ________
19. S s ________
20. T t ________
21. U u ________
22. V v ________
23. W w ________
24. X x ________
25. Y y ________
26. Z z ________

Name ______________________ Date ______________

B. Write the matching capital or lowercase letter.

Example: L l

1. B ____
2. x ____
3. n ____
4. Q ____
5. o ____
6. V ____
7. y ____
8. F ____
9. s ____
10. I ____
11. r ____
12. D ____

C. Circle the group of letters in each row that are in the correct order of the alphabet.

Example: k, d, t, u / (d, k, t, u)

1. o, d, y, r / d, o, r, y
2. g, n, q, x / q, n, x, g
3. b, d, g, i / g, d, i, b
4. w, u, s, k / k, s, u, w
5. m, n, o, p / p, n, o, m
6. s, u, j, e / e, j, s, u
7. c, l, y, v / c, l, v, y
8. u, n, a, z / a, n, u, z

D. Look at the words. Write the words in the order of the alphabet.

Example: teacher, student, classmate classmate, student, teacher

1. principal, nurse, school ______________________
2. flag, teacher, map ______________________
3. morning, afternoon, evening ______________________
4. Sara, Pedro, Jade ______________________
5. Lee, Bautista, Garcia ______________________

Name ______________________________ Date ________________

Vocabulary

Classroom Objects

Use with student book pages 18–19.

backpack	**dictionary**	**pen**
bag	**eraser**	**pencil**
book	**notebook**	

A. Look at the picture. Find the word below to match it. Write the letter next to the picture.

Example:  b

4.  ___

1.   ___

5.  ___

2. 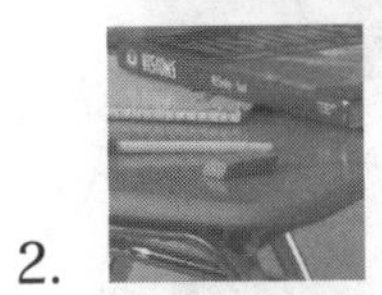 ___

6.  ___

3.  ___

7.  ___

a. pen	e. backpack
~~b. dictionary~~	f. book
c. pencil	g. eraser
d. notebook	h. bag

B. Write the word that goes with each picture.

Example:  bag

1.   ____________

3.  ____________

2. 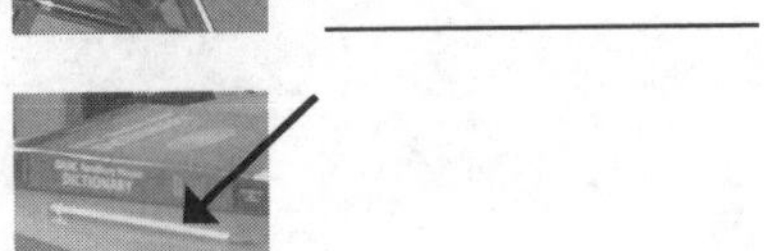 ____________

4. 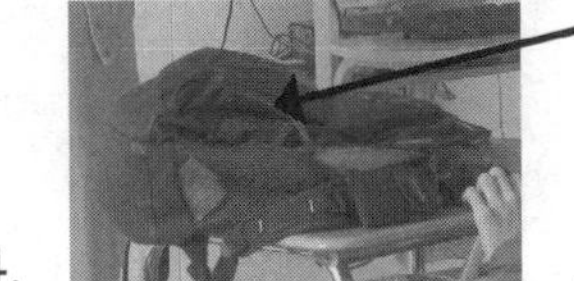 ____________

Name ______________________ Date ______________

Listening and Speaking

Talking About Possessions

Use with student book pages 20–21.

A. Finish this conversation.

Is this your pen?

Example: Yes, it is. Thanks.

1. You're ______________________.

Is that your bag?

2. No, ______________________.
3. Oh, ______________________.

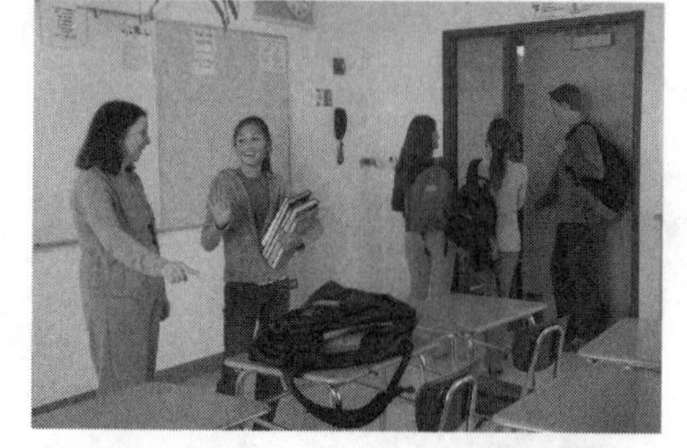

4. Is that your ______________________?
5. Yes, ______________________.

B. Do you have these possessions? Write your answers in the chart.

Possessions	Yes	No
Example: pen	Yes, I do.	
1. notebook		
2. backpack		
3. eraser		
4. marker		
5. book		
6. dictionary		
7. bag		

Name ________________________ Date ________________

C. Finish this conversation.

Excuse me. Do you have a dictionary?

Example: Yes, ___I do.___.

1. Thank ________________.

Excuse me. Do you have an eraser?

2. No, ________________.

3. That's ________________.

D. Finish the conversation. Use the phrases from the box.

Example: Is that your ___eraser___?

___Yes___, it is.

Questions
Is that
Excuse me. Do you have

Answers
Yes
No

1. Juan: ________________ your book?

   Maria: ________________, it is.

2. Juan: ________________ a pen?

   Maria: ________________, I don't. Sorry.

3. Juan: ________________ a pencil?

   Maria: ________________, I do.

Name ______________________ Date ______________

Listening and Speaking

Use with student book pages 22–23.

Counting Objects

A. Unscramble the word for each number.

Example: hetre
three

1. vife ______________
2. ixs ______________
3. tigeh ______________
4. noe ______________
5. ent ______________
6. nevse ______________
7. wto ______________
8. inne ______________
9. ehret ______________
10. uofr ______________

B. Write the numbers that come before and after the number you see.

Example: one, two, three

1. ______________, five, ______________
2. ______________, nine, ______________
3. ______________, one, ______________
4. ______________, four, ______________
5. ______________, eight, ______________

C. Draw the correct number of things.

one notebook	four bags	six erasers
three books	two backpacks	eight pencils

Name ______________________ Date ______________

D. Finish the conversation.

Example: Excuse me. Are these your books?

1. Yes, ______________________.

2. You're ______________________.

Are those your bags?

3. No, ______________________.

4. Oh, ______________________.

E. Finish the sentences. Use the words from the box.

Example: Are these your books?

Yes, they are.

~~they are~~	~~books~~
they aren't	pencils
my pencils	bag
my bag	it is

1. Juan: Is this your ______________?

   Maria: Yes, ______________.

2. Juan: This is ______________.

   Maria: Are these your ______________?

3. Juan: No, ______________.

   Maria: These aren't ______________.

Name ______________________________ Date ____________________

Letters and Sounds

Use with student book pages 24–25.

Vowel: Short a

A. Write the letter **a** in the word where it belongs. Say the word aloud when you write it.

Example:  b <u>a</u> g

1.  b ___ ckpack
2.  cl ___ ssroom
3.  m ___ p
4.  m ___ n
5.  f ___ mily
6.  c ___ p
7.  fl ___ g
8.  b ___ g

B. Circle the picture that goes with the word.

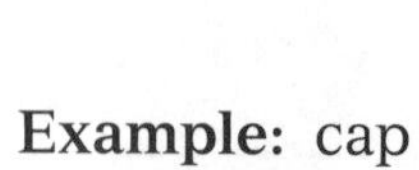

Example: cap  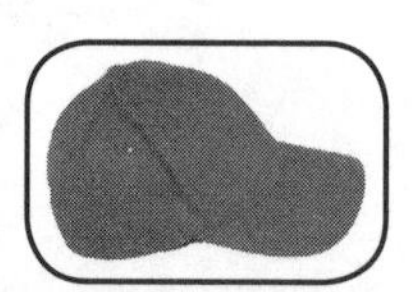

1. flag 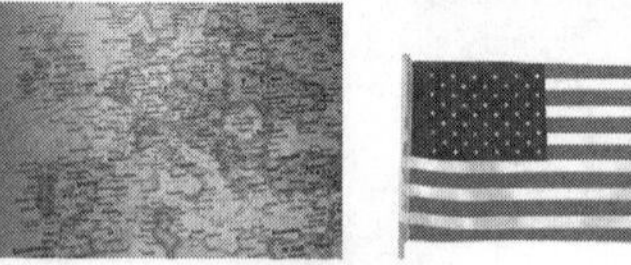
2. bag 
3. family  
4. classroom  

Name ______________________________ Date ____________________

A. Find the words from the box. Circle the words.

bag	backpack	cap	classroom	family	flag	man	map

x	v	r	m	w	i	o	s	j	k
b	c	l	a	s	s	r	o	o	m
q	a	e	p	l	s	t	h	l	c
m	p	h	q	b	w	a	u	q	z
q	d	j	w	o	a	f	l	a	g
d	f	i	f	a	m	i	l	y	x
r	t	l	v	l	i	d	f	z	v
y	b	a	g	p	k	l	r	x	m
h	r	m	c	t	p	l	w	k	a
b	a	c	k	p	a	c	k	y	n

B. Write the words.

1. __________

2. __________

3. __________

5. __________

4. __________

Name ______________________ Date ______________

Writing

Use with student book page 27.

A. Copy each sentence.

Example: This is my bag. This is my bag.

1. Is this Sara's pencil? ______________________
2. My name is Pam. ______________________
3. That is Jin Lee's book. ______________________
4. Are those your pens? ______________________

B. Read the sentences. Correct the sentences. Use capital letters.

Example: ~~i~~ I have a book.

1. what's in your backpack?
2. My name is jade.
3. do you have a dictionary?
4. no, I don't.
5. i have four notebooks.
6. that is my family.
7. is that your cap?
8. how many pens do you have?

C. Add the correct punctuation at the end of each sentence.

Example: That is my backpack _._

1. Are these Jin Lee's pencils _
2. Trang has five caps _
3. Do you have an eraser _
4. Are these your books _
5. Yes, I have a backpack _
6. Is this your family _

Name ______________________ Date ______________

Vocabulary

Personal Information

Use with student book pages 30–31.

address	state
apartment number	street
city	zip code
phone number	

A. Write the word for each piece of information.

Example: 15 Mission Street address

1. CA ______________
2. (661) 555-3428 ______________
3. Apt. 3B ______________
4. Bakersfield ______________
5. 93301 ______________

B. Unscramble the word for the piece of information.

Example: sddraes address

1. mnae ______________
2. izp odce ______________ ______________
3. tiyc ______________
4. astet ______________
5. epnho ubnemr ______________ ______________
6. pantmerat bnmrue ______________ ______________
7. dsasder ______________

Name ______________________ Date ______________

Listening and Speaking
Telling Your Age

Use with student book pages 32–33.

A. Draw a line from the word to the number.

Example: twelve — e. 12

1 twenty-one	a. 21
2. thirty	b. 100
3. sixteen	c. 80
4. one hundred	d. 40
5. forty	e. 12
6. sixty	f. 60
7. nineteen	g. 14
8. eighty	h. 16
9. fourteen	i. 30
10. fifty	j. 19
	k. 50

B. Say and write the missing number.

Example: 18, 19, 20

1. 50, 51, ____
2. 30, 31, ____
3. 14, ____, 16
4. ____ 94, 95
5. 25, ____, 27
6. 38, 39, ____
7. ____, 61, 62
8. ____, 12, 13
9. 75, 76, ____
10. 82, ____, 84

C. Write the number for the word.

Example: forty-five 45

1. one hundred ____
2. twenty-six ____
3. fifty-five ____
4. ninety-nine ____
5. forty-two ____
6. seventeen ____
7. eighty-seven ____
8. thirty-one ____
9. seventy-three ____
10. sixty-four ____

Name ______________________ Date ______________

D. Write the word for each number.

Example: 15 fifteen

1. 96 ______________
2. 11 ______________
3. 23 ______________
4. 81 ______________
5. 72 ______________
6. 44 ______________
7. 65 ______________
8. 59 ______________
9. 18 ______________
10. 37 ______________

E. Write the number from the box in each sentence.

16	20	35	62

Example: Jack is 35 years old.

1. May is _____ years old.
2. Waseem is _____ years old.
3. Tanya is _____ years old.

F. Write each sentence again. Use the number for the number word.

Example: I'm sixteen. I'm 16.

1. I'm twenty-nine. ______________
2. He's sixty-two. ______________
3. She's one hundred. ______________
4. I'm fifty-six. ______________
5. She's ninety-three. ______________

Name ______________________ Date ______________

Listening and Speaking

Saying Addresses

Use with student book pages 34–35.

A. Circle the correct way to write the number.

Example: three-six-two-nine	2638	4519	(3629)
1. seven-four-two-eight	6519	7428	8347
2. nine-one-one-five	9115	1519	5999
3. eight-six-three-four	6487	8634	3795
4. five-nine-seven-one	1175	5971	9874
5. four-three-eight-two	8283	4382	3428

B. Match the two numbers.

Example: six-four-three-five	a. nine twenty-eight
1. nine-two-eight	b. fifteen eighty-five
2. seven-seven-six-six	c. sixty-four thirty-five
3. eight-one-four	d. seventy-seven sixty-six
4. one five eight five	e. eight fourteen

C. Write the numbers for the zip code.

Example: two-three-six-nine-three 23693

1. one-nine-zero-zero-one ______________
2. nine-three-nine-two-seven ______________
3. four-three-two-five-three ______________
4. six-oh-two-oh-one ______________
5. seven-six-five-nine-nine ______________
6. zero-two-three-three-three ______________
7. one-oh-one-nine-oh ______________
8. five-seven-seven-six-zero ______________

Name ______________________ Date ______________

D. Write the words for the number.

Example: six-oh-four 604

1. seven thirty-eight ____________
2. twenty-nine eighteen ____________
3. three-three-five-six ____________
4. fifty-eight forty-one ____________
5. nine-nine-two-seven ____________
6. six-six-oh ____________
7. one ninety-three ____________
8. five thirteen ____________

E. Circle **yes** if the words and numbers match. Circle **no** if the words and numbers do not match.

Example: one-four-seven-five	1475	(**yes**)	**no**
1. three-five-six-seven-four	35674	**yes**	**no**
2. seven-five-one-three-nine	85128	**yes**	**no**
3. one-oh-one	110	**yes**	**no**
4. two-four-six	256	**yes**	**no**
5. eight sixty-two	862	**yes**	**no**
6. nine twenty-one	912	**yes**	**no**
7. three-one-oh	310	**yes**	**no**
8. one seventy-one	171	**yes**	**no**

Name ______________________________ Date ______________________

Letters and Sounds

Use with student book pages 36–37.

Initial Consonants: d, j, l
Final Consonants: d, l

A. Say the word for the picture. Write the beginning letter.

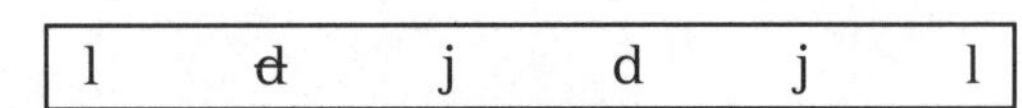

Example: d 

2. ____ 

4. ____ 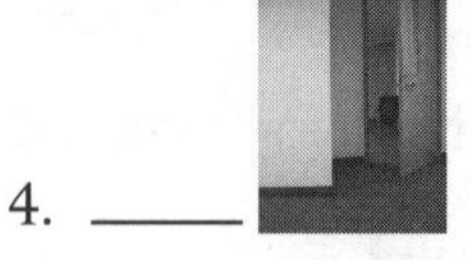

1. ____ 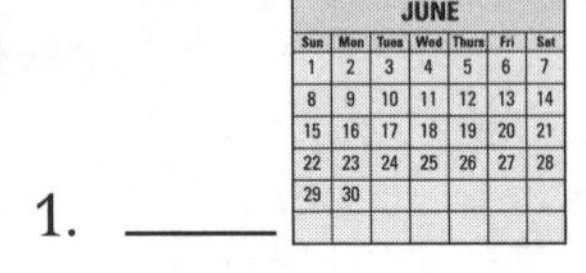

3. ____ 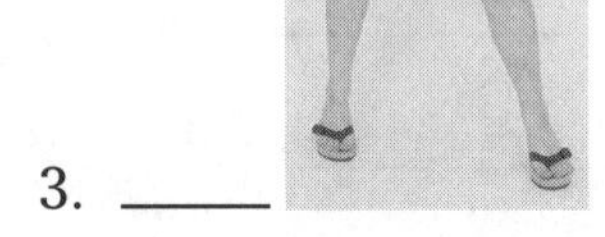

5. ____ 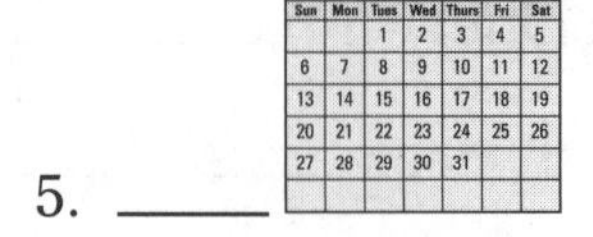

B. Say the word for the picture. Write the last letter.

Example:  hea d

2. 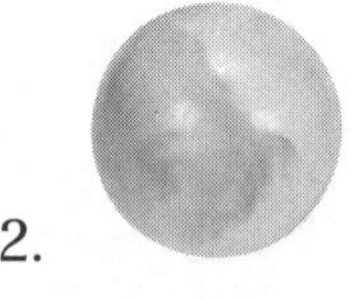 bal____

1. boar____

3. penci____

C. Circle the words that begin with the same sound.

Example: desk 

1. leaf door leg
2. June door desk
3. July leaf June
4. desk leg door

Name ______________________ Date ______________

D. Write the word for each picture in the crossword puzzles.

Example:

H			
E			
A			
D	E	S	K

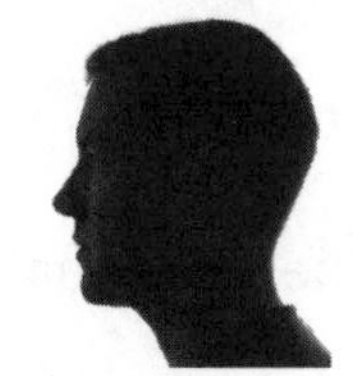

1. 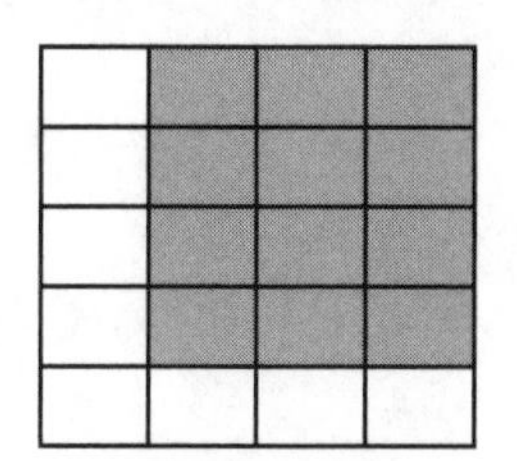

2. 

3. 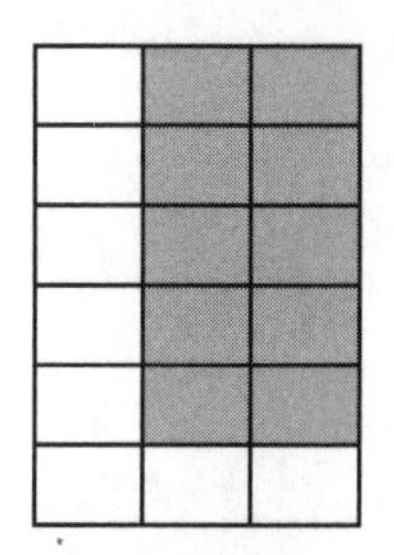

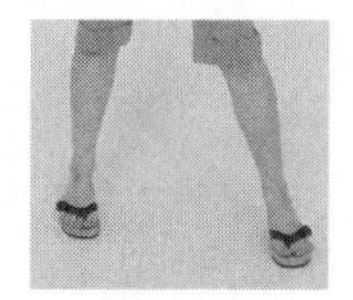

4. 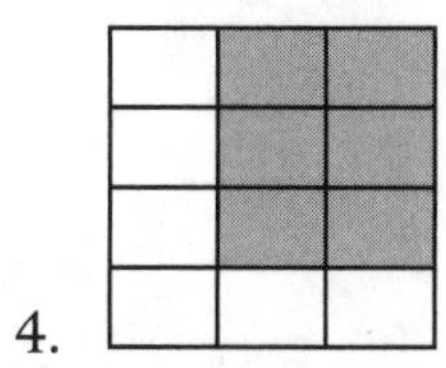

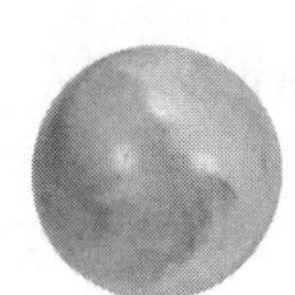

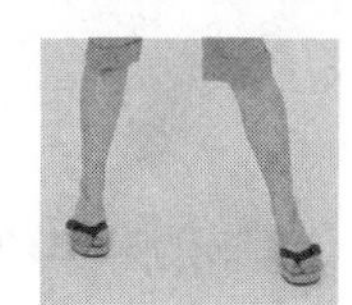

E. Draw a picture for each sentence.

Dad is sad.	The cap is for Al.
Pat has a cat.	The jam is for Dad.

Name ______________________________ Date ____________________

Letters and Sounds

Use with student book pages 38–39.

Initial Consonants: n, r, v
Final Consonants: n, r, x

A. Say the word for the picture. Circle the word that starts with the same letter.

Example: 9	pencil	address	(name)
1.	family	ride	cap
2.	van	teacher	bag
3.	name	pen	girl
4.	fan	eraser	read
5. 9	notebook	principal	state
6. 	dictionary	violin	school

B. Say the word for the picture. Circle the last letter in the word.

Example:  (n) r x

1.  n r x

2.  n r x

3.  n r x

4. n r x

5.  n r x

Name ______________________ Date ______________

C. Say each word. Circle the word that starts with a different letter.

Example: nine (back) number nurse

1. violin	fan	vacuum	van
2. run	radio	read	cat
3. school	nine	name	notebook
4. vat	dictionary	van	violin
5. rat	ran	red	six

D. Unscramble each word. Then draw a picture for the sentence.

Example: The man has a (aodri). radio

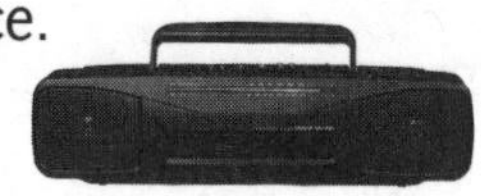

1. Jan has a (rca). __________

2. I have (nnie) pencils. __________

3. This is Sara's (inovli). __________

4. The cat is in the (obx). __________

Name ______________________ Date ______________

Writing

Introducing Yourself

Use with student book page 41.

A. Write about yourself.

Example: My name is Sara Jones.

1. My name is ______________.
2. I am from ______________.
3. I am ______________ years old.
4. I go to ______________ school.
5. I live in ______________, ______________.
6. ______________ is my English teacher.

B. Write about a classmate. Circle **She** or **He.**

Example: Ana Martinez is my classmate. (She) / He is from Colombia.

1. ______________ is my classmate.
2. She / He is from ______________.
3. She / He ______________ is years old.
4. She / He goes to ______________ school.
5. She / He lives in ______________, ______________.
6. ______________ is his / her English teacher.

C. Circle the sentence that uses capital letters correctly.

Example: I'm from sacramento, california. / (I'm from Sacramento, California.)

1. He lives in park city, utah. / He lives in Park City, Utah.
2. Her address is 9735 Maple Street. / Her address is 9735 maple street.
3. She's from Vietnam. / She's from vietnam.
4. My school is on Washington avenue. / My school is on Washington Avenue.
5. I'm from philadelphia, pennsylvania. / I'm from Philadelphia, Pennsylvania.

Name ______________________ Date ____________

Vocabulary

Classroom Language

Use with student book pages 44–45.

board	**computer**	**light switch**	**workbook**
chair	**desk**	**picture**	
classroom	**door**	**piece of paper**	

A. Write the word for each picture.

Example: 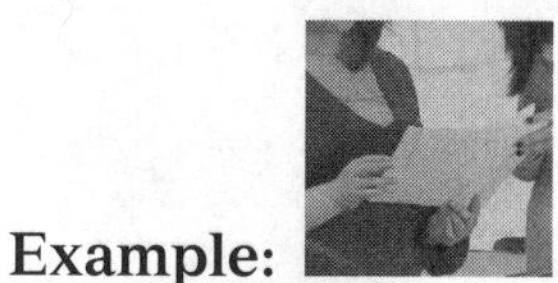 piece of paper

1.  ______________

2. ______________

3.  ______________

4.  ______________

5. ______________

6. ______________

7.  ______________

8.  ______________

9.  ______________

10.  ______________

B. Unscramble these words.

Example: esdk desk.

1. pcmtureo ______________
2. kbrwkooo ______________
3. dbaro ______________
4. hirac ______________
5. socalroms ______________
6. orod ______________
7. witshc gihlt ______________
8. itpruec ______________

Name ______________________________ Date ____________________

Listening and Speaking

Classroom Activities

Use with student book pages 46–47.

A. Circle the sentence that tells about the picture.

Example: Erase the board. (Close the door.)

1. Sit down. Close your bag.
2. Stand up. Open your notebook.
3. Write your address. Stand up.
4. Take out a pencil. Turn on the computer.

B. Complete the sentences. Use words from the box. Use each word one time.

Example: ____Draw____ a picture of your dog.

Close	~~Draw~~	Erase	Open	Take out
Turn on	Turn off	Stand	Sit	Write

1. ____________________ your address in your notebook.
2. ____________________ your dictionary to page 54.
3. ____________________ the words from the board.
4. ____________________ a piece of paper.
5. ____________________ the computer.
6. ____________________ your book.
7. ____________________ the lights.
8. ____________________ up from your desk.
9. ____________________ down in your chair.

Name ______________________ Date ______________

C. Use the words to make a sentence.

Example: notebook. / Close / your Close your notebook.

1. dictionary. / your / Take out

____

2. Erase / sentence. / the

____

3. a / car. / a / of / Draw / picture

____

4. number. / your / Write / phone

____

5. notebook. / your / Open

____

D. Circle the words to finish each sentence.

Example: Take out (your address / a pen).

1. Draw a picture of (a house / a zip code).
2. Open (the pencil / your dictionary).
3. Erase (the board / your bag).
4. Close (the sentence / your book).

E. Write a word from the box to complete each sentence. Draw a picture to go with your sentence.

Example: Open your notebook

address	computer	~~notebook~~	pencil	picture

1. Turn off the __________.
2. Draw a __________ of your family.
3. Write your __________.
4. Take out your __________ and paper.

Name ______________________ Date ______________

Listening and Speaking

Use with student book pages 48–49.

Describing and Asking for Objects

A. Match each picture with the correct word.

Example:

1. 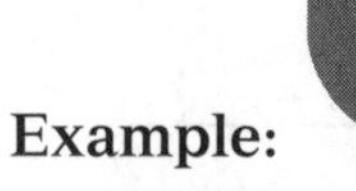
2. 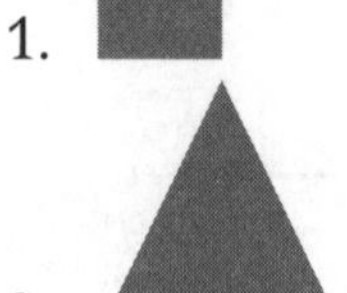
3. 
4. 
5. 
6. 
7. 

a. a small square

b. a large rectangle

c. a large square

d. a large triangle

e. a large circle

f. a small triangle

g. a small circle

h. a small rectangle

B. Complete the sentences. Use the words from the box.

~~small~~	square	triangle	large

Example: This is a ___small___ rectangle.

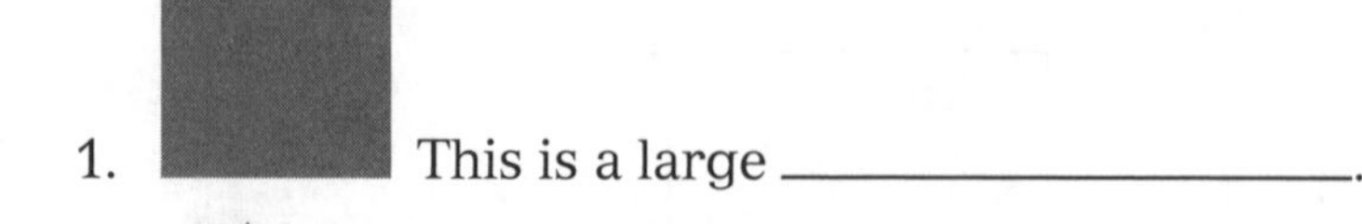

1. This is a large ______________.
2. This is a small ______________.

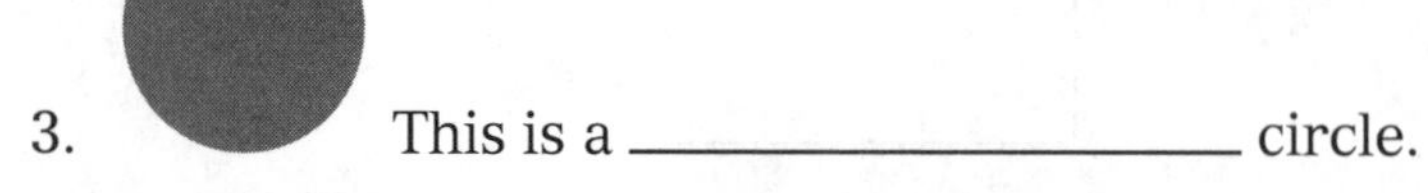

3. This is a ______________ circle.

Name ______________________ Date ______________

C. Write a size word and a shape word to describe each shape.

Example: 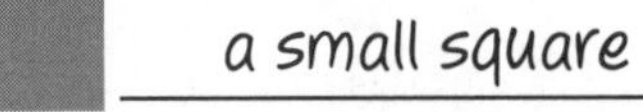

Size Words	Shape Words
large	circle
small	rectangle
	square
	triangle

1.  a ______________
2.  a ______________
3. 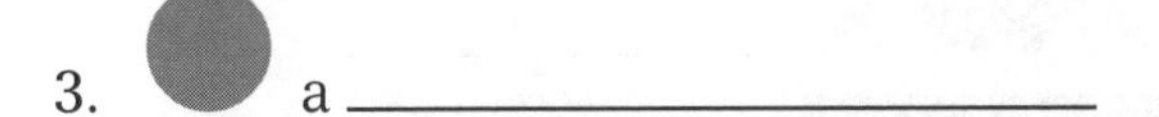 a ______________
4. a ______________
5.  a ______________
6. 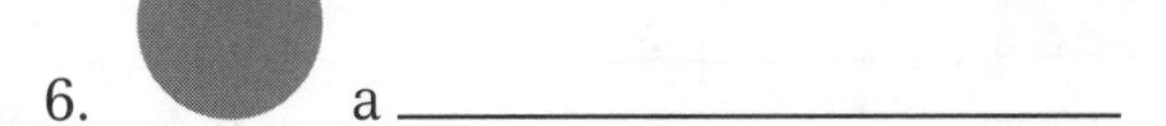 a ______________

D. Read the sentence. Draw a picture.

Example: Draw a large black square.

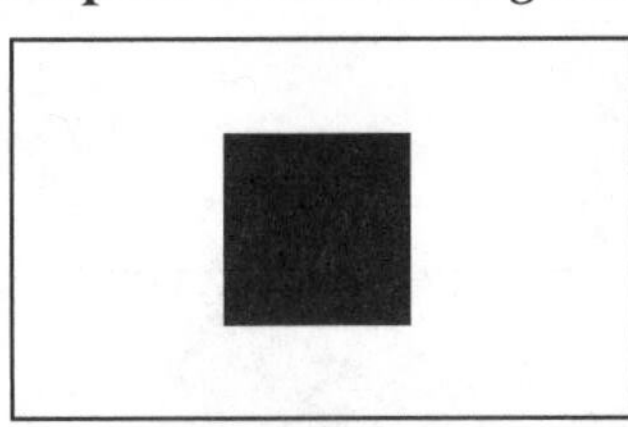

1. Draw a small green car.

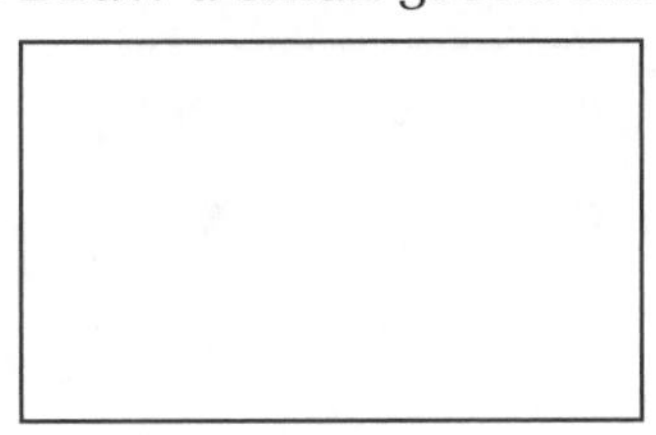

2. Draw a small brown dog.

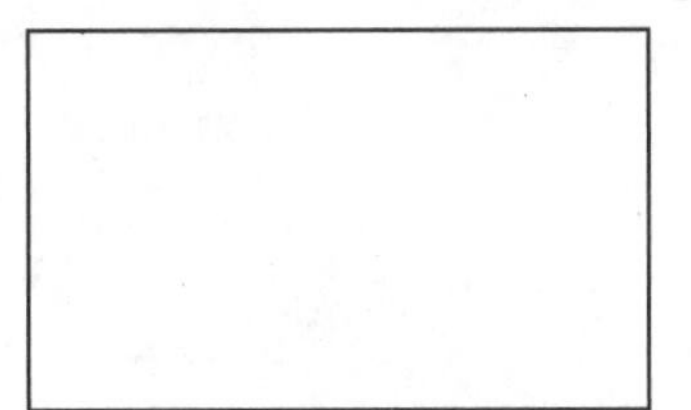

3. Draw a large red box.

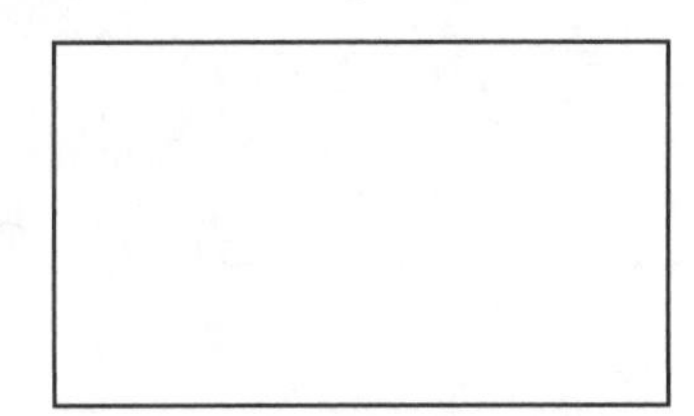

4. Draw a large yellow sun.

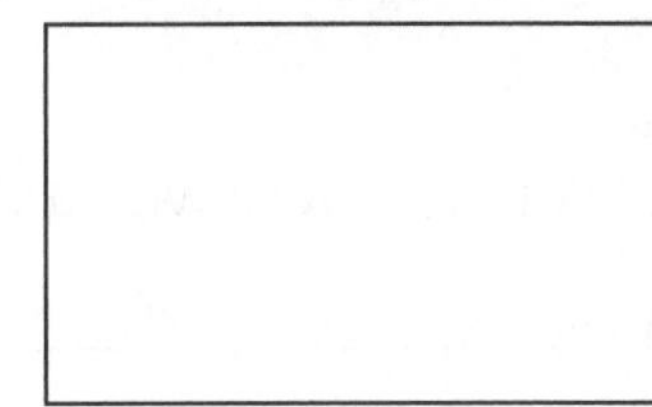

5. Draw a small orange triangle.

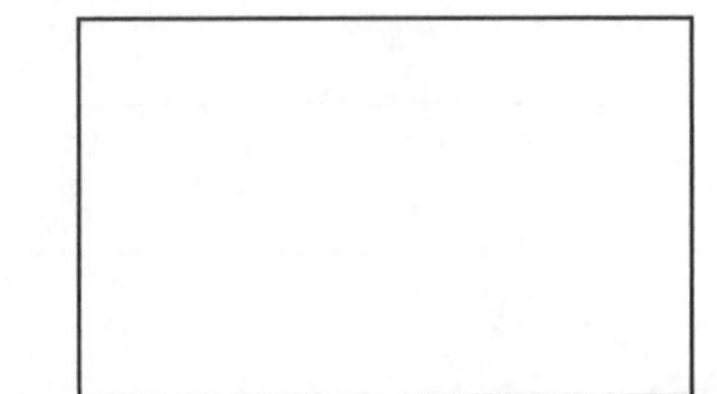

Name ______________________ Date ______________

Letters and Sounds

Vowel: Short o

Use with student book pages 50–51.

A. Write the word for each picture.

Example: mop

box	clock	doll	hockey
locker	~~mop~~	pot	rock

1. ______________________

2.  ______________________

3.  ______________________

4. ______________________

5. ______________________

6. 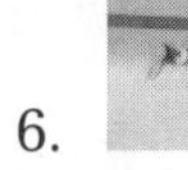 ______________________

7. 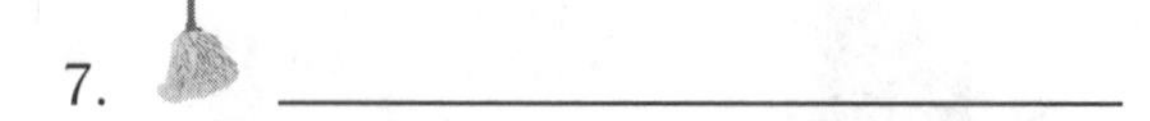 ______________________

8. ______________________

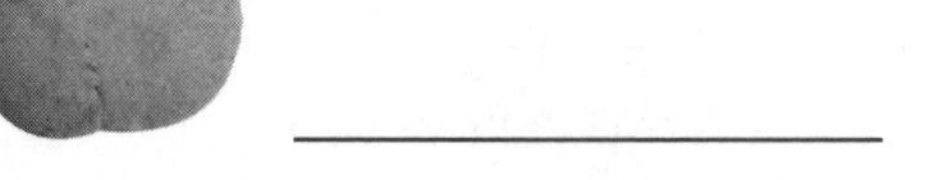

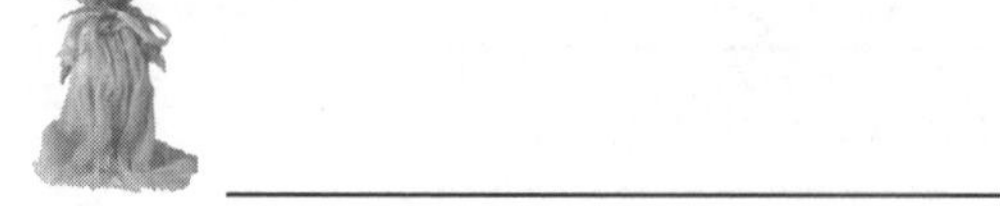

B. Say the words. Write the word with a different vowel sound.

Example: box bag sock bag

1. mat pot ham ______________________
2. rock sack sock ______________________
3. mop pop map ______________________
4. clack clock rock ______________________
5. bat hot cap ______________________

Name ______________________ Date ______________

C. Change the letter **a** to the letter **o.** Write the new word.

Example: tap top

1. map ______________
2. pat ______________
3. rack ______________
4. sack ______________
5. hat ______________

D. Read the sentences. Draw a picture to go with each sentence.

Example: I have a mop and a clock.

1. I have a doll and a bag.
2. The cat is on the rock.
3. The clock is in the classroom.
4. There is a cap in the locker.

E. Read the sentences. Unscramble the word in parentheses.

Example: I like to play (yekcoh). hockey

1. My little (llod) is in my backpack. ______________
2. The red bag is in the (cokerl). ______________
3. These books are in the (xob). ______________
4. This (lckco) is a circle. ______________
5. The big (tpo) is in the bag. ______________

Name ______________________ Date ______________

Writing

Use with student book page 53.

Describing Flags

A. Read these sentences. Put commas where they belong.

Example: The flag of Cambodia is red, white, and blue.

1. The American flag is red white and blue.
2. The flag of Mexico is green white and red.
3. The Cuban flag is red white and blue.
4. The flag of Afghanistan is black red and green.
5. The Brazilian flag is green yellow blue and white.
6. The flags of China Cuba and Somalia have stars.
7. The flags of Russia the United States of America and Cuba have stripes.
8. The flags of Vietnam Brazil China and Mexico have yellow on them.
9. The Brazilian Afghan and Mexican flags have green on them.
10. The Chinese Vietnamese and Somalian flags do not have stripes.

B. Write three words from the box to finish the sentences. Put commas where they belong. You can use the words more than one time.

black	blue	brown	green	orange
purple	red	white	yellow	

Example: My pencils are blue, purple, and orange.

1. I have ____________, ____________, and ____________ caps.
2. I like ____________, ____________, and ____________ cars.
3. They have ____________, ____________, and ____________ backpacks.
4. My friends have ____________, ____________, and ____________ pens.
5. I have ____________, ____________, and ____________ bags.

Name ______________________ Date ______________

Vocabulary
School Subjects

Use with student book pages 56–57.

art	math	physical education / P.E.	social studies
language arts	music	science	

A. Look at each book. Write the word for the school subject.

Example: 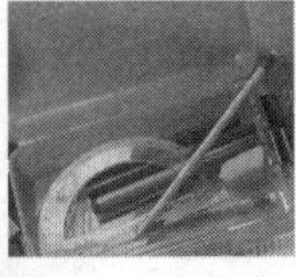 art

1. 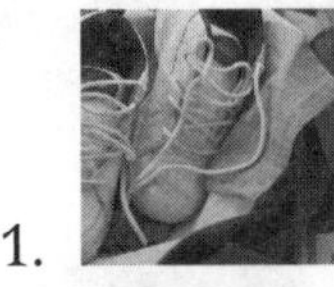 ______________
2. 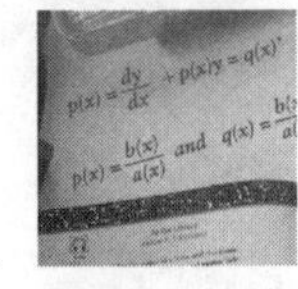 ______________
3.  ______________
4.  ______________
5. 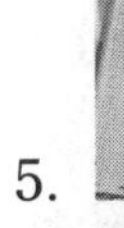 ______________
6.  ______________

B. Draw a picture. Show something about each school subject.

1. science

2. art
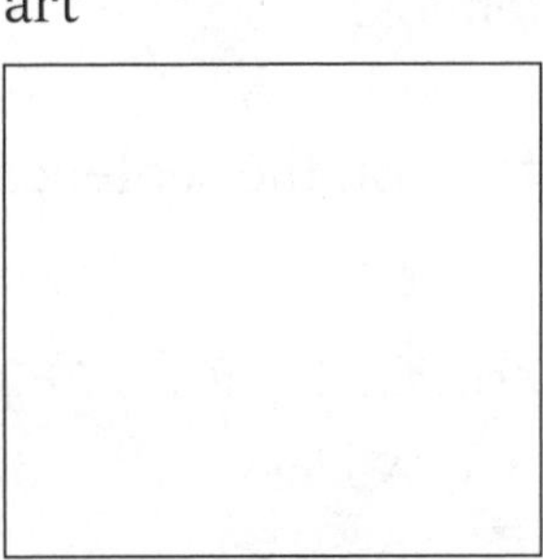
3. language arts
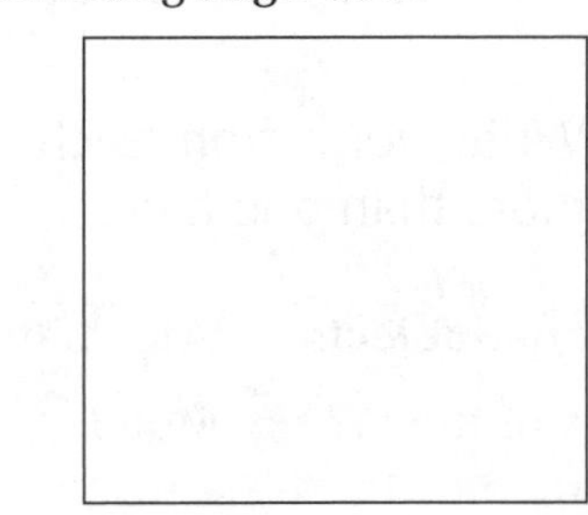
4. physical education / P.E.
5. math
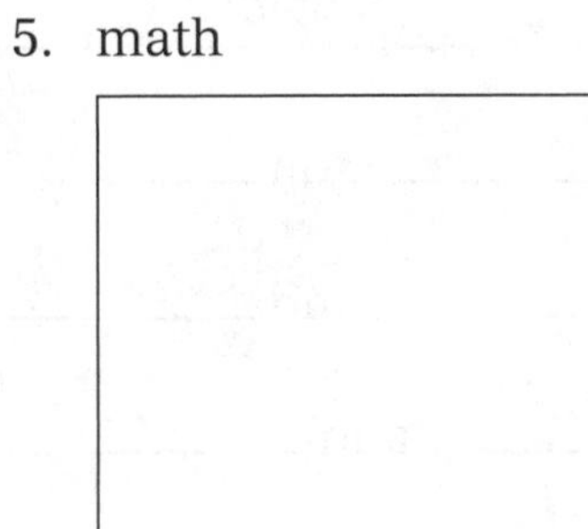
6. social studies
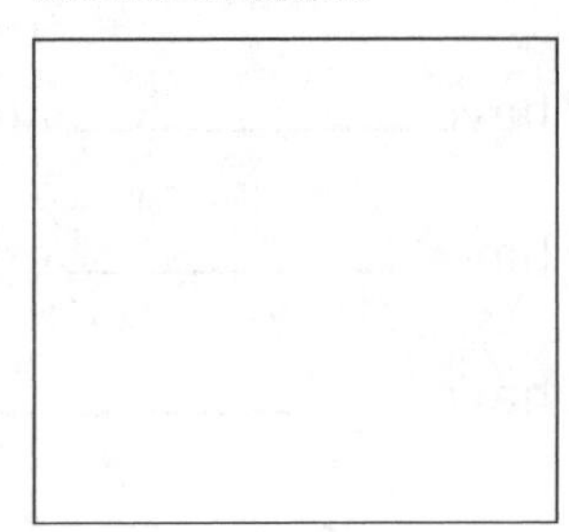

Name ______________________ Date ______________

Listening and Speaking

Use with student book pages 58–59.

Talking About Classes

A. Read the question. Circle the sentence that answers the question.

Example: Do you have art class?

(Yes, I do.)

I have science class on Friday.

1. What classes do you have on Monday?

   He does not have music and math.

   I have language arts, science, and P.E.

2. When do you have math and art?

   I have them on Tuesday, Wednesday, and Thursday.

   Pedro has social studies on Monday, Thursday, and Friday.

3. Do you have language arts class?

   My music notebook is in my backpack.

   Yes, I do.

4. What classes do you have on Tuesday?

   No, I don't.

   I have language arts, math, and science.

5. Do you have social studies on Wednesday and Thursday?

   No, I don't.

   I have a social studies notebook.

B. Write words from each box to finish the sentences. You can use the words more than one time.

School Subjects	art, language arts, math, music, P.E., science, social studies
Days of the Week	Monday, Tuesday, Wednesday, Thursday, Friday, Saturday, Sunday

Example: I have ___art___ and ___music___ on ___Tuesday___.

1. I have __________ and __________ on __________.

2. I have __________ on __________ and __________.

3. I have __________, __________, and __________ on __________.

4. I do not have __________ on __________.

Name ______________________ Date ______________

C. Match the day with the abbreviation.

Example: Wednesday — b. Wed.

1. Monday	a. Sun.
	b. Wed.
2. Friday	c. Fri.
3. Tuesday	d. Mon.
4. Saturday	e. Sat.
5. Thursday	f. Thurs.
6. Sunday	g. Tues.

D. Write the abbreviation for the day.

Example: I have science class on Thursday. Thurs.

1. Trang has P.E. class on Monday. ______________
2. Jin Lee has language arts class on Friday. ______________
3. I don't have music class on Saturday. ______________
4. Sara has social studies class on Tuesday. ______________
5. They have math class on Thursday. ______________
6. I have an art class on Sunday. ______________
7. Pedro doesn't have art class on Wednesday. ______________

E. Write the word or abbreviation for the missing day.

Example: Monday, Tuesday, Wednesday

1. ______________, Fri., Sat.
2. Sunday, ______________, Tuesday
3. Wed., Thurs., ______________
4. ______________, Tuesday, Wednesday
5. Tuesday, ______________, Thursday
6. ______________, Sunday, Monday
7. Sunday, Monday, ______________
8. Fri., Sat., ______________

Name ______________________________ Date ____________________

Listening and Speaking

Talking About Schedules

Use with student book page 60.

A. Read the schedule. Answer the questions.

Monday	Tuesday	Wednesday	Thursday	Friday
language arts	language arts	language arts	language arts	language arts
P.E.	social studies	art	social studies	P.E.
math	math	science	science	math

Example: When do you have art? I have art on Wednesday.

1. When do you have P.E.?

____

2. When do you have language arts?

____

3. When do you have math?

____

4. When do you have social studies?

____

5. When do you have science?

____

B. Read each sentence. Fill in the schedule.

Example: I have art on Tuesday.

1. I have social studies on Monday and Friday.
2. I have language arts on Wednesday and Thursday.
3. I have physical education on Monday, Tuesday, Wednesday, and Thursday.
4. I have art on Tuesday.
5. I have music on Friday.
6. I have math on Monday, Tuesday, and Wednesday.
7. I have science on Thursday and Friday.

Monday	Tuesday	Wednesday	Thursday	Friday
	art			

Name ______________________ Date ______________

Listening and Speaking

Months of the Year

Use with student book page 61.

A. Match the month and the abbreviation.

Example: February — a. Aug.

1. April — b. Oct.
2. June — c. Apr.
3. August — d. Dec.
4. October — e. Jun.
5. December — f. Feb.

B. Write the correct abbreviation for each month.

Example: February — Feb. Fe. feb Febr — Feb.

1. November — novm Nov. Nove novemb. ______
2. May — May my. M. ma ______
3. September — sepr Sept SE. Sept. ______
4. January — ja. Jany. janu Jan. ______
5. March — Mar. MA. mrch mar. ______
6. July — J. ju Jul. JY ______

C. Write the word or abbreviation for the missing month.

Example: January, February, March

1. May, June, ______
2. Sept., ______, Nov.
3. ______, February, March
4. November, ______, January
5. Mar., ______, May
6. ______, September, October

Name ______________________ Date ______________

Letters and Sounds

Vowel: short i

Use with student book pages 62–63.

A. Say the word for the picture. Circle the word with the same short vowel sound.

Example: 6 fox (fix) fax

1. hat hit hot
2. an in on
3. box family dinner
4. fifty backpack hockey

B. Read the words in the box. Write the word for each picture.

Example: 50 fifty

dinner	~~fifty~~	inch	kitchen	milk	nickel	six	window

1. ______________
2. ______________
3. 6 ______________
4. ______________
5. ______________
6. ______________

C. Read each word. Change the vowel to **i.** Write and say the new word.

Example: max mix

1. pot ______________
2. bag ______________
3. sat ______________
4. lap ______________

Name ______________________________ Date ____________________

D. Make more words. Write a different letter from the box.

b c d f g j l m p s t

Example: six → f ix   si t

1. pin → ___ in   pi ___
2. lip → ___ ip   li ___
3. rid → ___ id   ri ___
4. sit → ___ it   si ___
5. fix → ___ ix   fi ___

E. Unscramble each word. Draw a line from the word to the picture.

Example: (irndne) dinner

1. (xis) ______________
2. (ckitnhe) ______________
3. (icnlke) ______________
4. (cinh) ______________
5. (ftiyf) ______________
6. (ilmk) ______________
7. (inwwdo) ______________

a.

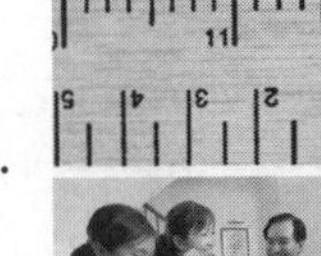
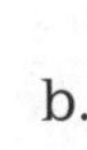
b.

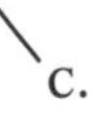
c.

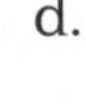
d.

e.

f.

g.

h.

Name ______________________ Date ______________

Letters and Sounds

Initial Consonants: h, k, q, w, y, z

Use with student book pages 64–65.

A. Write the letter from the picture that goes with each word.

Example: hand j

1. quarter ____
2. yellow ____
3. kitchen ____
4. key ____
5. water ____
6. zipper ____
7. question ____
8. window ____
9. yogurt ____
10. house ____
11. zero ____

a. 

e.  

i. 

b. 

f. 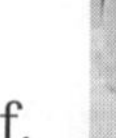 

j.  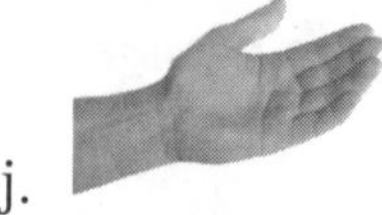

c. 

g. 

k. 

d.

h.

l.

B. Write the missing letter.

Example: Here is my h ouse.

1. I have four ___ uarters.
2. The ___ ogurt is made from milk.
3. My bag has a big, red ___ ipper.
4. Our school has many ___ indows.
5. There is a ___ ey for the door.
6. Is this your ___ ouse?
7. The clock is in the ___ itchen.
8. The ___ ater is in the big pot.
9. I have a ___ uestion—is this your bag?
10. There is a pencil in your ___ and.

Name ______________________________ Date ________________

C. Say the word for each picture. Circle the word that begins with the same sound.

Example:  (hit) bag

1. ? quilt box
2.  clock win
3.  yam tap
4. 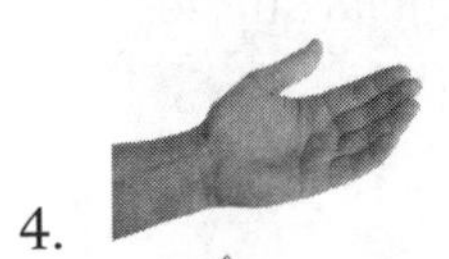 doll hat
5.  kit pink
6. 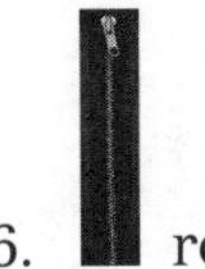 rock zag
7.  yes mop
8.  orange kid
9.  hockey cap
10.  man win
11.  zip red
12.  cat quick

D. Match the words that start with the same letter.

Example: house	a. question
1. kitchen	b. window
2. quarter	c. hand
3. water	d. zipper
4. yellow	e. key
5. zero	f. yogurt

Name ______________________ Date ______________

Writing

Writing Your School Schedule

Use with student book page 67.

School Schedule

	Mon.	Tues.	Wed.	Thurs.	Fri.
Class 1	language arts	language arts	language arts	language arts	language arts
Class 2	music	art	music	art	art
Class 3	math	math	math	math	math
Class 4	lunch	physical education	lunch	physical education	lunch
Class 5	physical education	lunch	physical education	lunch	music
Class 6	science	science	science	social studies	social studies

A. Finish the sentence about the schedule.

Example: Class 1 on Monday is language arts.

1. Class 4 on Tuesday and Thursday is ______________.
2. I have math every day for Class ______________.
3. I do not have art on ______________ and ______________.
4. I have science on ______________, ______________, and ______________ for Class ______________.

B. Write these sentences again. Use uppercase letters.

Example: Pedro has art on thursday and friday.
Pedro has art on Thursday and Friday

1. Mr. Allen teaches social studies on thursday and friday.

____

2. We have language arts on monday, tuesday, wednesday, thursday, and friday.

____

Name ______________________________ Date ________________

Vocabulary

My Favorite Things

Use with student book pages 70–71.

actor	CD	game	sports
baseball team	food	movie	TV show
basketball player			

A. Write the word for each picture.

Example:  basketball player

1.  ______________
2. ______________
3.  ______________
4. ______________
5.  ______________
6.  ______________
7.  ______________
8.  ______________

B. Draw a picture. Show something about each thing.

1. CD

2. food

3. sports

Name ________________________ Date ____________

Listening and Speaking

Talking About Likes

Use with student book pages 72–73.

A. Circle the words that belong in the group.

Example: Kinds of food: (pasta) classical basketball (soup)

1. Kinds of music: pop soccer chicken rock
2. Kinds of sports: salad basketball fruit baseball
3. Kinds of food: chicken hip-hop football pizza
4. Kinds of music: Chinese food hip-hop baseball classical
5. Kinds of sports: soccer football rock fish

B. Write the word that answers each question.

Example: What kind of music do you like?

(baseball / classical) I like classical.

1. What kind of food do you like?
   (pizza / baseball) I like ____________.
2. What kind of music do you like?
   (chicken / rock) I like ____________.
3. What kind of sports do you like?
   (fruit / basketball) I like ____________.
4. What kind of food do you like?
   (hip-hop / fruit) I like ____________.
5. What kind of music do you like?
   (pop / football) I like ____________.
6. What kind of sports do you like?
   (salad / soccer) I like ____________.

Name ______________________________ Date ______________

C. Read the chart. Read the questions. Write answers to the questions.

Name	Food	Music	Sports
Sara	Chinese food	pop	basketball
Jade	Mexican food	classical	baseball
Mark	Korean food	rock	soccer
Alberto	Cuban food	hip-hop	football

Example: What kind of music does Jade like?
Jade likes classical music.

1. What kind of food does Mark like?
____

2. What kind of sports does Alberto like?
____

3. What kind of food does Sara like?
____

4. What kind of music does Mark like?
____

5. What kind of sports does Jade like?
____

D. What do your classmates like? Ask questions. Write the words in the chart. Write sentences.

Classmate's Name	Food	Music	Sports
Luis	pizza	hip-hop	soccer

Example: Luis likes pizza, hip-hop, and soccer.

1. ______________________________

2. ______________________________

Name ______________________ Date ______________

Listening and Speaking

Talking About Favorites

Use with student book pages 74–75.

A. Read the questions. Use a sentence from the box to answer each question.

I like it a lot.	It's OK.	I don't like it very much.

Example: Do you like rock music? I like it a lot

1. Do you like basketball? ______________________
2. Do you like hip-hop music? ______________________
3. Do you like pizza? ______________________
4. Do you like fish? ______________________
5. Do you like pop music? ______________________

B. Circle the word that answers the question.

Example: What's your favorite food? My favorite food is (basketball / (pizza)).

1. What's your favorite sport? My favorite sport is (fish / soccer).
2. What's your favorite food? My favorite food is (fruit / hip-hop).
3. What's your favorite music? My favorite music is (chicken / classical).
4. What's your favorite sport? My favorite sport is (baseball / soup).
5. What's your favorite music? My favorite music is (rock / salad).

C. Write a question. Use the word in parentheses.

Example: (sport) What's your favorite sport?

1. (singer) ______________________
2. (actor) ______________________
3. (TV show) ______________________
4. (sports team) ______________________

Name ______________________ Date ______________

D. Read each question. Write an answer for each question.

Example: What's your favorite food?

My favorite food is salad.

1. What's your favorite music?

2. What's your favorite movie?

3. Who's your favorite singer?

4. What's your favorite CD?

5. Who's your favorite basketball player?

6. What's your favorite TV show?

7. Who's your favorite music group?

8. What's your favorite song?

9. What's your favorite movie?

10. Who's your favorite actor?

Name ______________________ Date ______________

Letters and Sounds

Use with student book pages 76–77.

Vowel: short u

A. Say the word for each picture. Circle the word with the same short vowel sound.

Example:  pen pan (pun)

1.  but bat bet
2.  lack lick luck
3.  jig jag jug
4.  lug lag leg

B. Read the words in the box. Write the word for the picture.

bus	cup	lunch	sum	sun	~~umbrella~~	brush

Example:  umbrella

1. 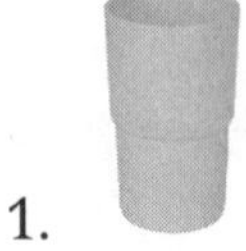 ______________
2. 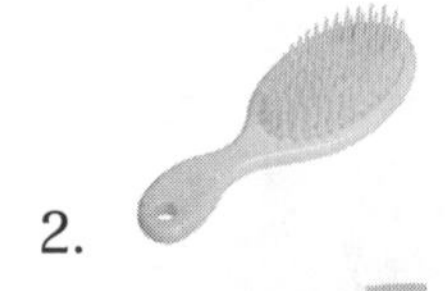 ______________
3.  ______________
4.  ______________
5.  ______________
6. 2 + 2 = 4 ______________

C. Read each word. Change the vowel to **u**. Write the new word.

Example: ran run

1. bat ______________
2. bag ______________
3. doll ______________
4. him ______________
5. mist ______________
6. rib ______________
7. cat ______________
8. cap ______________

Name ______________________ Date ______________

D. Unscramble each word. Draw a line from the word to the picture.

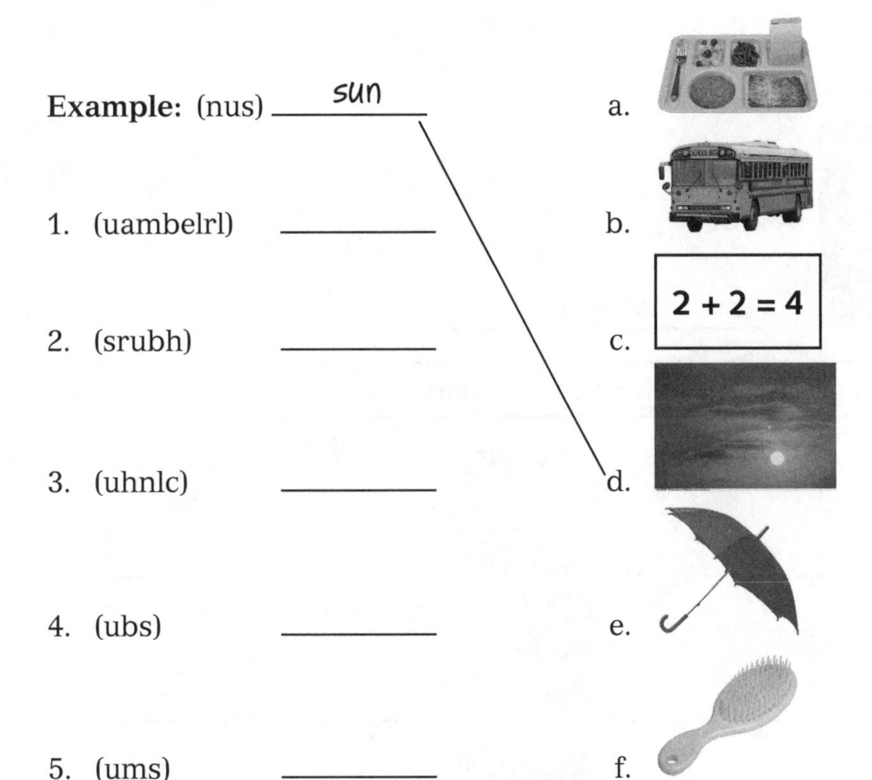

Example: (nus) sun — a.

1. (uambelrl) ________ — b.
2. (srubh) ________ — c.
3. (uhnlc) ________ — d.
4. (ubs) ________ — e.
5. (ums) ________ — f.

E. Say the words. Write the two words with the short **u** vowel sound.

Example: box buck bat bus — buck — bus

1. bud ball bet brush ________ ________
2. clock cub cup crib ________ ________
3. launch lunch lack luck ________ ________
4. snag sum snug swim ________ ________
5. number hockey kitchen truck ________ ________
6. sand six sun suds ________ ________
7. locker umbrella dinner jump ________ ________
8. inch brush skunk window ________ ________

Name ______________________ Date ______________

Letters and Sounds

Vowel: short e

Use with student book pages 78–79.

A. Write the word for each picture.

Example: 

address

pen	leg	exit	desk	~~address~~	ketchup	tennis	neck

1. ______________
2.  ______________
3.  ______________
4. 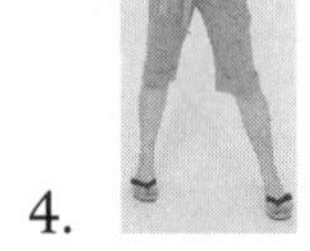 ______________
5. ______________
6. 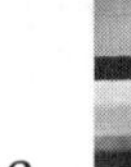 ______________
7.  ______________

B. Read the words in the box above. Circle each word in the puzzle.

k	e	t	c	h	u	p
q	r	t	e	x	i	t
p	e	n	a	d	v	e
r	l	e	g	g	j	n
l	c	c	x	w	d	n
p	s	k	b	n	e	i
a	d	d	r	e	s	s
q	r	l	m	c	k	v

Name ______________________________ Date ________________

C. Say the word for each picture. Circle the word that has the same vowel sound.

Example: (net) not

1. them thin
2. and end
3. set sat
4. vet vat
5. chick check
6. rod red
7. pig peg

D. Read each sentence. Circle the words in each sentence that have the short **e** sound. Draw a picture to go with the sentence.

Example: I have a (pen) and a (desk).

1. I play tennis with Ned.
2. The pen is on the desk.
3. I like red ketchup on my eggs.
4. Ben and Beth go out the exit.

Name ______________________ Date ______________

Writing

Use with student book page 81.

Writing About Your Favorites

Finish each sentence about yourself. Then use this page to make your Web site.

Example: I like ____rock____ music a lot.

About Me

Hi. My name is ______________.

I am from ______________.

I am ______________ years old.

Music

I like ______________ music a lot.

My favorite singer is ______________.

He / She's ______________.

Sports

I like ______________ a lot.

My favorite team is ______________.

I like ______________ and ______________, too.

Food

I like ______________ food.

My favorite food is ______________.

I like ______________ and ______________, too.

School Subjects

I go to ______________ School.

My favorite subject is ______________.

I am good at ______________ and ______________, too.

Name ______________________________ Date ______________

Vocabulary

Around the School

Use with student book pages 84–85.

nurses' office	**library**	**restrooms**
gymnasium	**cafeteria**	**auditorium**
music room	**stairs**	

A. Unscramble the words.

Example: (smiymnaug) gymnasium

1. (urnses' ficoef) ______________
2. (udmitoariu) ______________
3. (tsarsi) ______________
4. (ibryalr) ______________
5. (mestroors) ______________
6. (afteercia) ______________
7. (mcusi ormo) ______________

B. Write the correct word from the vocabulary list to finish each sentence.

Example: You wash your hands in the restrooms.

1. You eat lunch in the ______________.
2. You play sports in the ______________.
3. You go to the ______________ if you are sick.
4. You go up and down the ______________.
5. You listen to the principal in the ______________.
6. You read books in the ______________.
7. You study music in the ______________.

Name ______________________ Date ______________________

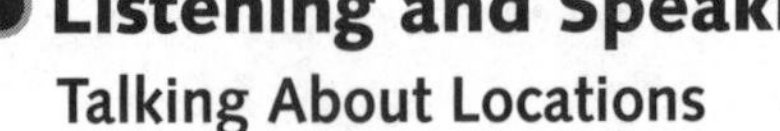

Listening and Speaking

Talking About Locations

Use with student book pages 86–87.

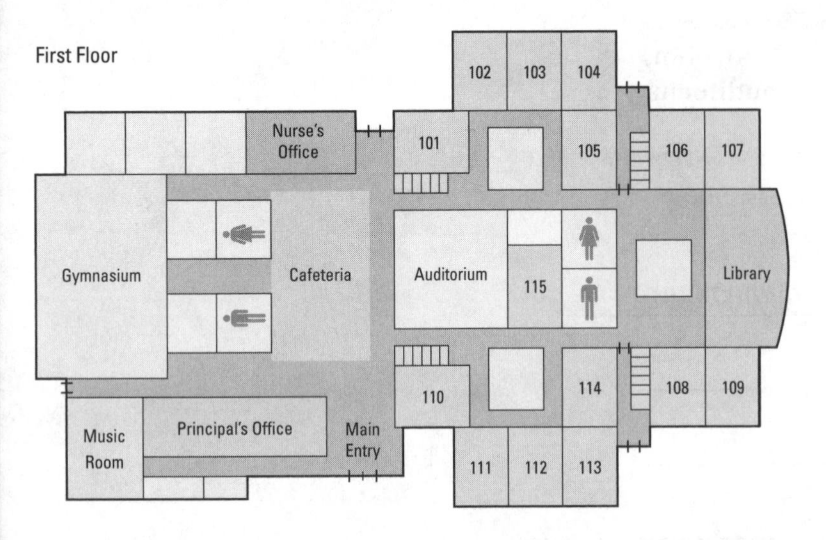

~~cafeteria~~	principal's office	library
music room	stairs	gymnasium

A. Look at the map. Write a word from the box to finish each sentence.

Example: The nurse's office is across from the cafeteria.

1. The principal's office is next to the ______________.
2. The ______________ is across from the music room.
3. The main entry is next to the ______________.
4. The ______________ is between Room 107 and Room 109.
5. The ______________ are next to Room 106.

B. Look at the map above. Read each question. Write **yes** or **no** to answer the question.

Example: Is the gymnasium next to the library? no

1. Is the music room next to the principal's office? ______________
2. Is the library on the second floor? ______________
3. Is the auditorium between Room 101 and Room 110? ______________

Name ______________________ Date ______________

C. Look at the map. Draw a line to match the place and the location.

Example: The cafeteria
1. The music room
2. The library
3. Room 114
4. The auditorium

a. is across from the gymnasium.
b. is between Room 107 and Room 109.
c. is next to Room 113.
d. is between the nurse's office and the principal's office.
e. is across from Room 110.

D. Look at the map. Write an answer for each question.

Example: Excuse me. Where's the restroom?
The restroom is next to the cafeteria.

1. Excuse me. Where's the music room?
____
2. Excuse me. Where's the principal's office?
____
3. Excuse me. Where's the restroom?
____
4 Excuse me. Where's the library?
____
5. Excuse me. Where are the stairs?
____
6. Excuse me. Where is Room 112?
____
7. Excuse me. Where is the auditorium?
____
8. Excuse me. Where is the nurse's office?
____

Name ______________________ Date ______________

Listening and Speaking

Giving Directions

Use with student book pages 88–89.

A. Look at the map. Read each question. Circle the correct answer.

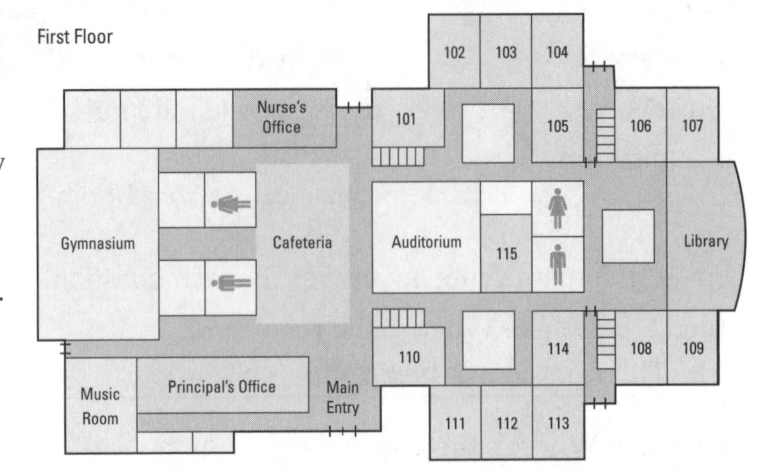

Example: Excuse me. How do I get from the music room to the cafeteria?

a. Go left at the library. It's next to Room 108.

(b.) Go right. It's across from the principal's office.

1. Excuse me. How do I get from the library to the stairs?
   a. Go right. They're between Room 105 and Room 106.
   b. Go straight down the hallway. They're next to Room 115.
2. Excuse me. How do I get from the auditorium to the library?
   a. Go left at the principal's office. It's across from the music room.
   b. Go right and then go straight down the hallway. It's across from the restrooms.
3. Excuse me. How do I get from the Room 114 to the gymnasium?
   a. Go right. It's across from the stairs.
   b. Go left. Go straight down the hall. It's on the right.

B. Look at the map. Write directions.

Example: Go from the cafeteria to the nurse's office. *Go across the hall.*

1. Go from Room 115 to the library.

   ____

2. Go from Room 114 to Room 107.

   ____

3. Go from the auditorium to the girls' restroom.

   ____

Name ______________________ Date ______________

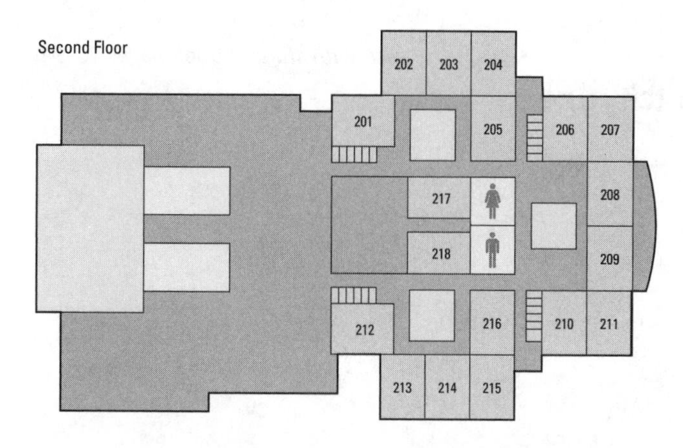

C. Look at the maps. Write **yes** or **no** to answer each question.

Example: Is the gymnasium on the second floor? ___no___

1. Do I go to the second floor for the nurse's office? ______________

2. Is there a girls' restroom on the second floor? ______________

3. Are the stairs between Room 210 and Room 216? ______________

4. Is Room 203 between Room 205 and Room 204? ______________

5. Do I go to the first floor to get to the library? ______________

D. Look at the maps. Write the directions.

Example: How do I get from Room 211 to the auditorium?

Go down the stairs next to Room 210. Go left. Go down the hallway. The auditorium is on the right.

1. How do I get from Room 212 to the nurse's office?

____

____

2. How do I get from Room 217 to Room 103?

____

____

3. How do I get from Room 209 to the library?

____

____

Name ____________________ Date ____________

Letters and Sounds
Digraphs: sh, ch; Trigraphs: tch, dge

Use with student book pages 90–91.

A. Draw a line from the picture to the word.

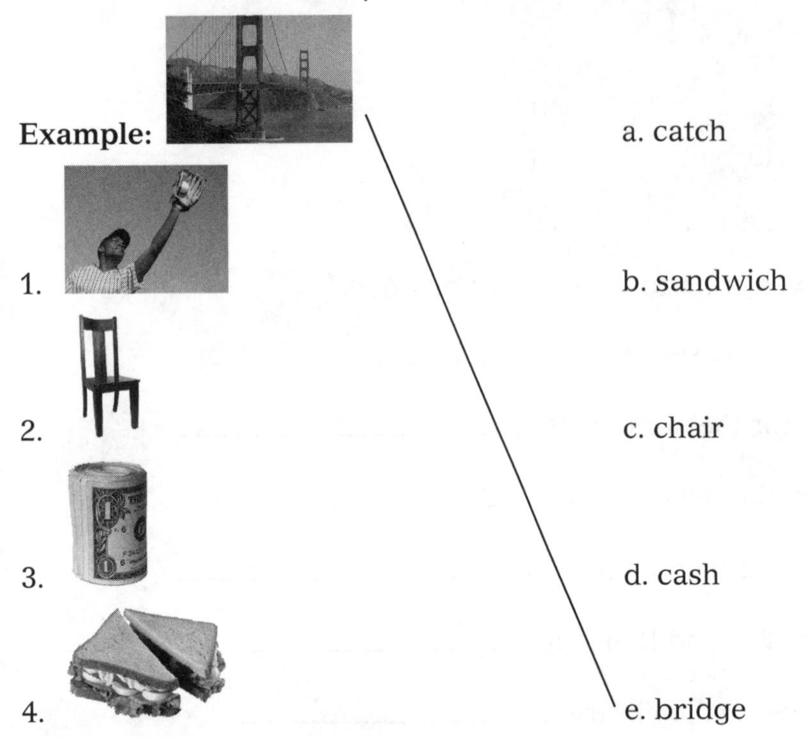

Example: e. bridge

1. a. catch
2. b. sandwich
3. c. chair
4. d. cash

B. Say the words. Write the two words that start with the same sound.

Example: shirt hockey ship locker shirt ship

1. bus show nickel shoes __________ __________
2. chip dinner chair pizza __________ __________
3. window flag chick chin __________ __________
4. classroom shop desk shirt __________ __________

C. Say the words. Write the two words that end with the same sound.

Example: sandwich cap March flag sandwich March

1. family catch locker patch __________ __________
2. principal judge fudge classroom __________ __________
3. fifty March backpack porch __________ __________
4. board violin badge edge __________ __________

Name ______________________________ Date ______________

D. Say the word for each picture. Write **sh, ch, tch,** or **dge** to complete the word.

Example: ca tch

1.  ba ______
2.  wa ______
3. 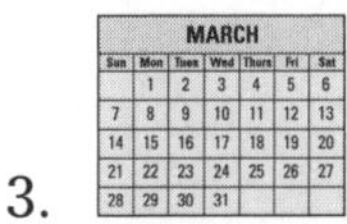

Mar ______
4.  fi ______
5.  ______ irt
6. 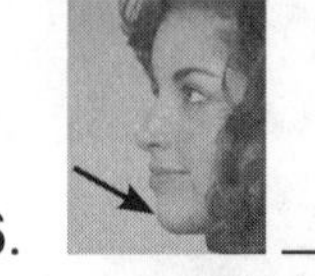 ______ in
7.  pa ______
8.  ju ______
9.  ca ______
10.  ______ air
11. 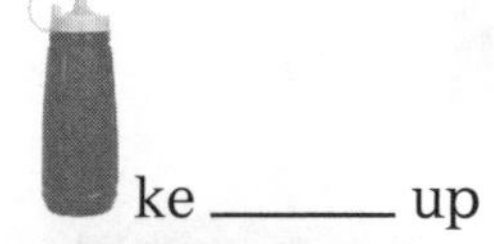 ke ______ up
12.  he ______

E. Circle each word that has **sh, ch, tch,** or **dge** in it.

Example: Ben has a (patch) on his (chin).

1. Put on your shirt and your watch.
2. Which shoes match your pants?
3. Catch the ball before it gets to the hedge.
4. Push back. You're at the edge of the ledge!
5. Do you like ketchup on your cheese sandwich?
6. I got my fish for five dollars in cash.
7. The policeman showed his badge to the judge.
8. We went over the bridge last March.

F. Look at your answers from Exercise E. Write each word in the box where it belongs.

sh	ch	tch	dge
	chin	patch	

Name ______________________ Date ______________

Letters and Sounds

Digraphs: th, ng, nk

Use with student book pages 92–93.

A. Say the word for each picture. Write the correct digraph.

Example: 30 __th__ irty
nk th

1.  ri ____
nk ng

2. 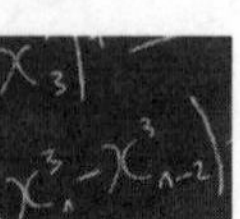 ma ____
nk th

3. 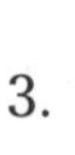  ____ umb
ng th

4.   dri ____
nk ng

5.  wi ____
th ng

6. 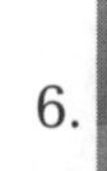  si ____
nk th

7.  si ____
th ng

8. 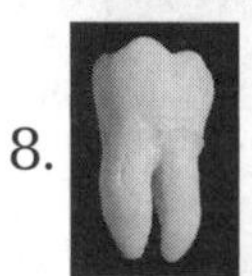 too____
nk th

9.   tru ____
nk ng

10.  ba ____
nk th

B. Unscramble each word.

Example: (bhumt) __thumb__

1. (inkg) ________ 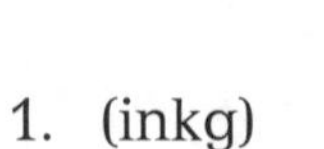 

2. (hotot) ________ 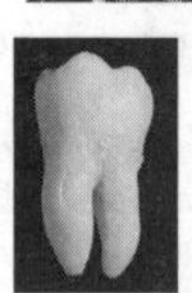

3. (krutn) ________ 

4. (abnk) ________ 

Name ______________________ Date ______________

C. Circle each word that has **th, ng,** or **nk** in it.

Example: (Beth thanked Hank) for the (ring).

1. Wink if you like the pink drink.
2. Put both of the cloths in the trunk.
3. Trang likes to sing with Seth.
4. Our teacher will bring thirty pencils to math class.
5. Mei Ling sang a long song.

D. Read your answers from Exercise C. Write each word in the correct box. Some words may go in more than one box.

th	ng	nk
Beth	ring	thanked
thanked		

E. Write a sentence for each word.

Example: (king) The United States of America does not have a king.

1. (thirty) ______________________
2. (ring) ______________________
3. (bank) ______________________
4. (wing) ______________________
5. (math) ______________________
6. (trunk) ______________________
7. (tooth) ______________________
8. (drink) ______________________

Name ______________________ Date ______________

Writing

Use with student book page 95.

Writing Directions

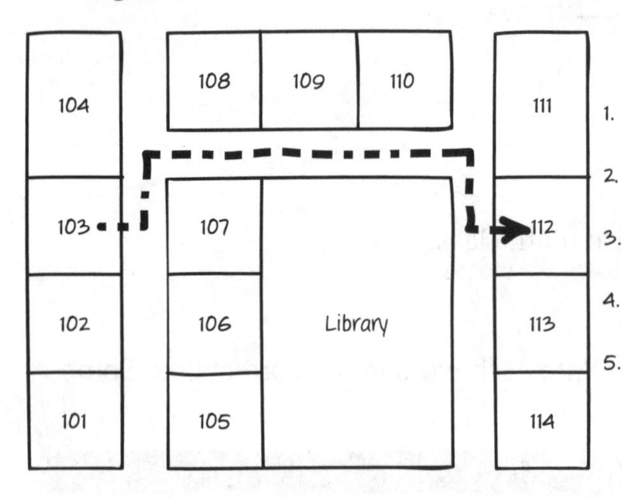

A. Look at the map. Write the room number to finish the sentence.

Example: Room ___109___ is between Room 108 and Room 110.

1. Room ________ is next to Room 101.
2. Room ________ is between Room 111 and Room 113.
3. Room ________ is across from Room 101.
4. Room ________ is next to Room 103 and across from Room 108.

B. Write directions.

Example: How do I get from Room 101 to Room 107?
Go left. Walk down the hall. Turn right after Room 106.

1. How do I get from Room 108 to the library?

____

2. How do I get from Room 114 to Room 111?

____

3. How do I get from Room 102 to Room 106?

____

4. How do I get from the library to Room 111?

____

Name ______________________________ Date ____________________

Vocabulary

Classroom Objects

Use with student book pages 102–103.

schedule	**cabinet**
calculator	**workbook**
ruler	**textbook**
computer and printer	

A. Write the correct classroom object for each picture.

Example: cabinet **1.** ____________ **2.** ____________ **3.** ____________

4. ____________ **5.** ____________ **6.** ____________

Welcoming a New Student

B. Fill in the blanks. Use the correct vocabulary words.

Teacher: Hello. My name is Ms. Miller. I'm your **(example)** teacher. (ecatrhe)

Student: Hello, Ms. Miller. Nice to meet you.

Teacher: Here are your books. This is your (1) ____________ (etkxobot) and your (2) ____________. (obkorokw)

Student: Thank you.

Teacher: We have a (3) ____________ (pormucte) and ____________. (irernpt) They are on the desk, next to the (4) ____________. (tibnace) In the cabinet, there is a (5) ____________ (rrleu) and a (6) ____________ for you. (llccaruato)

Name ______________________ Date ______________

Vocabulary

Use with student book pages 104–105.

Asking to Borrow Things

A. Look at the pictures. Complete the sentences with the correct Vocabulary word.

Example:
Alex: Excuse me. Do you have a class schedule?
Ms. Miller: Yes, I do.

1. **Tina:** Pablo, do you have a ______________?
   Pablo: Sure. Here you are.

2. **Jordan:** Excuse me. May I borrow a ______________?
   Olivia: Sorry. No, I don't have one.

3. **Mr. Miller:** Sam, do you have a ______________?
   Sam: Yes, I have one in my desk.

4. **Mary:** May I borrow a calculator?
   Mr. Perez: Yes, one is in the ______________.

Forms

B. Fill in Tasha's form with her information.

TashaSmith@email.com
(610) 222-1234
7921 Locust Street
Storrs, CT 06269
Tasha Smith

Name: ______________
Address: ______________
____
Phone Number: ______________
E-mail Address: ______________

Name ______________________ Date ______________

Grammar

Subjects and Verbs

Use with student book page 106.

The Verb *be*			
I	**am** a teacher.	We	**are** at school.
You	**are** a student.	You	**are** students.
He	**is** Toni.	They	**are** in the library.
She	**is** Maya.	They	**are** desks.
It	**is** a pen.		

A. Fill in the blanks with the correct form of the verb **be.**

Example: Alex Garcia ___is___ a student.

1. Ms. Miller __________ his teacher.
2. I __________ at home.
3. My brother __________ over there.
4. We __________ students.
5. You __________ in the United States.

B. Remember: A complete sentence needs a subject and a verb. Decide if these sentences are correct or not. Write correct if the sentence is correct. If it is not correct, write a correct sentence.

Examples: You in class. ___You are in class.___

They are students. ___correct___

1. Her name Ana Smith. __________
2. There is rulers and calculators on the desk. __________
3. I am a student. __________
4. Is in school. __________
5. You welcome. __________

Name ______________________ Date ______________

Grammar

Use with student book page 107.

Possessive Adjectives

Possessive Adjective	Sentence
my	I am a teacher. **My** name is Mr. Miller.
your	You are a student. **Your** teacher is Ms. Lopez.
his	He is from Colombia. **His** name is Pedro.
her	She is a nurse. **Her** office is in the school.
its	The cat is under the table. **Its** name is Bella.
our	We are in class. **Our** teacher is Mr. Miller.
their	They are from Russia. **Their** names are Ivan and Anna.

A. Fill in each blank with the correct possessive adjective. The pronouns are in parentheses ( ).

Example: This is ___my___ textbook. (I)

1. May I borrow __________ ruler? (you)
2. That is __________ brother. (she)
3. __________ computers are over there. (we)
4. That is __________ calculator on the table. (I)
5. __________ homework is in the workbook. (they)
6. He likes __________ schedule. (he)

B. Put the words in the correct order to make a sentence. Use correct capitalization and punctuation.

Example: (Juan / name / his / is) His name is Juan.

1. (dog / black / is / His) ______________________
2. (is / desk / calculator / His / on / the) ______________________
3. (fifty / Our / has / desks / classroom) ______________________
4. (not / work / printer / does / My) ______________________
5. (big / is / cat / My) ______________________
6. (ruler / Her / in / is / the / cabinet) ______________________

Name ______________________ Date ______________

Grammar Expansion

Possessive Pronouns

Possessive pronouns and possessive adjectives tell who or what something belongs to. Possessive adjectives come before a noun. Possessive pronouns come after the verb **be.**

Possessive Adjective	Possessive Pronoun	Sentence
my	mine	This is my workbook. The workbook is **mine.**
your	yours	Those are your textbooks. The textbooks are **yours.**
his	his	This is his calculator. The calculator is **his.**
her	hers	That is her printer. The printer is **hers.**
our	ours	That is our computer. The computer is **ours.**
their	theirs	This is their cabinet. The cabinet is **theirs.**

A. Answer the questions with the correct possessive pronoun. Use the possessive pronoun in parentheses.

Example: Whose dog is this? It is mine. (my)

1. Is this your red ruler? No, it is ________. (her)
2. Is that your teacher? No, she is ________. (his)
3. Whose new computer is this? It is ________. (their)
4. Is this your desk? Yes, it is ________. (my)

B. Put the words in the correct order.

Example: (Is / workbook? / my / that) Is that my workbook?

(mine. / No, / it is) No, it is mine.

1. (that / Is / teacher? / your) ________________

   (hers. / No, /she / is) ________________

2. (Whose / this? / is / ruler) ________________

   (mine. / is / It) ________________

3. (pencil? / that / her / Is) ________________

   (hers. / it / Yes, / is) ________________

4. (this? / is / printer / Whose) ________________

   (It / ours. / is) ________________

Name ______________________ Date ______________

Word Study

Use with student book pages 108–109.

Final Blends

A. Say the word for each picture. Write the last letters.

Example:  inse ct

1. 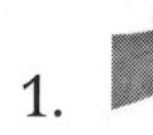  ha______
3.  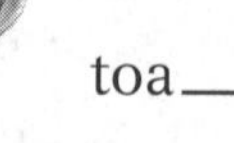 toa______
5.  gi______
2.  sa______
4. mi______
6. 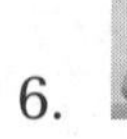 chi______

B. Read each word. Divide the word into beginning, middle, and end sounds. Keep the blends together.

Example: hand h / a / nd

1. nest __________
3. silk __________
5. dent __________
2. left __________
4. ramp __________
6. melt __________

C. Read each word. Look at the picture. Change the word to match the picture.

Examples:

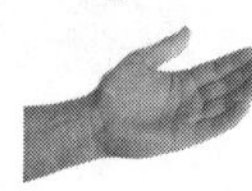 sand → hand

 elf → shelf

1.  silk → __________
3.  kelp → __________
2.  lift → __________
4. ramp → __________

D. Write the word for each picture. Circle the word in the puzzle.

Example:  elk

1.   __________
4.  __________
2.  __________
5.   __________
3. __________

y	z	s	a	l	t
s	h	e	l	f	m
w	e	g	h	i	i
q	l	v	b	t	l
k	p	d	o	s	k
c	h	i	l	d	u
d	e	l	k	o	p

Name ______________________ Date ______________

Word Study

Syllabication

Use with student book page 110.

A. Read each word. Put a check mark ✓ in the box that shows the number of syllables.

	1 syllable	2 syllables	3 syllables	4 syllables
Example: hand	✓			
1. textbook				
2. cabinet				
3. calculator				
4. student				
5. computer				
6. guardian				
7. pen				
8. study				

B. Divide the words into syllables.

Example: letter let / ter

1. computer ______________________
2. teacher ______________________
3. ruler ______________________
4. cabinet ______________________
5. printer ______________________
6. workbook ______________________
7. calculator ______________________
8. schedule ______________________

Name ______________________ Date ______________

Writing Assignment

Use with student book page 111.

Emergency Information Form

A. Correct the mistakes.

Example: oct30 2010 Oct. 30, 2010

1. ms jones ______________________
2. sept 6 2009 ______________________
3. mr miller ______________________
4. 2395 la brea st #12 ______________________
5. july 9 2015 ______________________

B. Read the paragraph. Then fill in the form. Use today's date.

Sara Maria Cream is in grade 3. Her teacher is Mr. Lopez. Her father is Tom Cream. His phone number is (213) 555-2343. His cell number is (213) 555-1013. Their address is 8 Judy Lane, Philadelphia, PA 19104.

School Emergency Information Form

Date: __________ **Grade:** ______ **Teacher:** ______________________

Name: ______________________________________

Last **First** **Middle**

Address: ______________________________________

Street

____

City **State** **Zip Code**

Parent or Guardian:

Name: ______________________

Phone: ______________________ **Cell:** ______________________

Name ______________________ Date ______________

Vocabulary From the Reading

Use with student book page 113.

Key Vocabulary

different	miss
friendly	nice
interesting	

A. Circle the correct Key Vocabulary word.

Example: My math teacher likes to smile. She is very (nice / interesting).

1. We play the piano in music class. It is (friendly / interesting).
2. My classmates like to help people. They are very (friendly / interesting).
3. Science class and history class are (different / friendly).
4. I keep in touch with my old classmates. I (don't miss / miss) them.

B. Complete the sentences with the correct Key Vocabulary word.

Example: Someone who helps people is nice.

1. Someone who likes to make friends is ______________.
2. Things that are not the same are ______________.
3. You want to see someone but you cannot. This is someone you ______________.
4. Something that you like to do or watch is ______________.

C. Fill in each blank with the correct Key Vocabulary word.

Monica: Ling, you are a new student from a **(example)** different school. What do you think of this school?

Ling: The teachers here are very (1)______________. And the classes are (2)______________. I learn many new things in each class.

Monica: Do you (3) ______________ your old classmates?

Ling: Yes, I do. But I like my new classmates, too. They are very (4)______________. I eat lunch and study with them every day.

Name ______________________ Date ______________

Reading Strategy

Scan for Information

Use with student book page 114.

You **scan** something to get **information** quickly.

Academic Vocabulary for the Reading Strategy		
Word	**Explanation**	**Sample Sentence**
scan	look quickly to find something	Joe **scans** the newspaper every day. He looks for the soccer scores.
information	facts or things you can learn about someone or something	Students write personal **information** on the form.

Here are the names and addresses of six friends.

Margie Thomas 12 Marilyn Road Phoenix, AZ 85003	Mr. John Miller 83 Nevers Road South Windsor, CT 06074	Sara Cream 8 Judy Lane Philadelphia, PA 19104
Luisa Zarco 1228 Novato Road San Rafael, CA 94903	Ms. Ana Lopez 2354 Sand Street Stony Brook, NY 11790	Tom Johnson 1812 Walker Avenue Apartment 2 Greensboro, NC 27412

Read each question. Scan the chart for information. Write the answer.

Example: What is Philadelphia's zip code? 19104

1. What street does Ms. Ana Lopez live on? ______________
2. Who lives on Judy Lane? ______________
3. Who lives in Phoenix? ______________
4. What is South Windsor's zip code? ______________
5. What is Sara's house number? ______________
6. What is Tom's apartment number? ______________
7. What road has house number 1228? ______________

Name ______________________ Date ______________

Text Genre

An Informal Letter

Use with student book page 114.

A letter is a message that you write on paper. An informal letter is to a friend or family member.

Informal Letter	
greeting	Dear *name*, ← commas
closing	Your friend, ←
signature	Luisa

Read this letter from José to his friend Antonio.

October 23, 2009

Hi! How are you? I'm fine. San Francisco is an interesting place. I love it here. The weather is nice. My grandmother says "hi." We miss you. Please write soon.

A. Write the three parts that are missing from the letter.

1. ______________________
2. ______________________
3. ______________________

B. Copy José's letter here. Write in the missing parts.

Name ______________________ Date ______________

Reading Comprehension

Use with student book page 116.

A. Answer the questions about the letter on page 115 in the student book.

Example: __a__ Who is Maggie?

a. (Luisa's friend) b. Ms. Douglas' daughter c. Luisa's sister

1. _____ Where is Luisa's old school?

   a. Florida b. Arizona c. California

2. _____ Where do some of Luisa's classmates come from?

   a. Mexico b. Australia c. Germany

3. _____ What does Luisa write about her class?

   a. cold b. bad c. interesting

4. _____ What does Luisa write about Ms. Douglas?

   a. good teacher b. bad friend c. friendly doctor

B. Answer the questions about Luisa.

Example: Does Luisa like San Rafael? __yes__

Where do you find the answer? __San Rafael is a nice place.__

1. Does Luisa like the people in San Rafael? ______________

   Where do you find the answer? ______________

2. Does Luisa find her classmates interesting? ______________

   Where do you find the answer? ______________

3. Does Luisa's teacher make class fun and interesting? ______________

   Where do you find the answer? ______________

4. Does Luisa want to see her old friends again? ______________

   Where do you find the answer? ______________

Name ______________________ Date ______________

Literary Element
Imagery

Use with student book page 117.

When a writer uses a lot of adjectives to describe a place, we can see that place in our mind. This is called imagery.

A. Circle the adjectives that use imagery.

Example: Dogs are (interesting) animals.

1. New York is an interesting place.
2. It is very fun.
3. The people here are friendly.
4. There are many different things to do.
5. My English teacher is very nice.
6. Her classmates are very friendly.

B. Choose a person, place, class, and game. Use imagery to write about them.

Example: (person) My sister is nice and friendly.

1. (person) ______________________

____

____

2. (place) ______________________

____

____

3. (class) ______________________

____

____

4. (game) ______________________

____

____

Name ______________________ Date ______________

Writing Conventions

Spelling: Irregular Sight Words

Use with student book page 117.

A. Unscramble the letters in parentheses ( ).

Example: ___Who___ is your new teacher? (ohW)

1. Mario ______________ the new student is friendly. (yass)
2. ______________ is your name? (Wath)
3. Ms. Douglas ______________ my teacher last year. (saw)
4. ______________ isn't Omar in class? (yhW)
5. His mother ______________ he is sick. (dais)
6. ______________ you late to class today? (reeW)

B. Circle the following words: **were, says, why, what, was, said,** and **who.** Words go up and down. Words go left to right.

W	H	I	D	W	E	R	N	L	S
E	A	B	C	D	Q	R	S	S	A
R	W	H	A	T	E	F	G	H	Y
E	T	V	V	I	W	A	S	A	S
W	X	S	U	J	K	L	W	O	U
Y	Z	A	X	M	W	H	Y	P	W
E	W	I	W	X	N	W	T	H	E
X	S	D	E	T	U	Y	V	Y	H
U	H	X	W	H	O	E	W	S	S
E	V	Y	W	S	X	Y	H	W	Z

Name ______________________ Date ______________

Vocabulary
School Events

Use with student book pages 122–123.

field trip	basketball game
school concert	pep rally
art show	school dance
graduation	a play
football game	

A. Write the correct Vocabulary word for each picture.

Example: field trip

1. ______________

2. ______________

3. ______________

4. ______________

5. ______________

Talking about School Events

B. Complete each sentence with a Vocabulary word. Not all Vocabulary words are used.

Example:
Juan: Do you like to dance?
Su Jin: Yes, I go to every school dance.

Dialogue #1
Pam: Our science class goes on a
(1) ______________
on the third of each month. We learn about animals.
Karen: I like to learn about animals. On November 15, I have a painting in the
(2) ______________.
It has six animals in it.

Dialogue #2
Jeff: I sing in the
(3) ______________
on December 20. Can you go?
Matsuo: I cannot go. My team has a
(4) ______________.
Before the game, there is a
(5) ______________.

Name ______________________ Date ______________

Vocabulary

Talking About Dates

Use with student book pages 124–125.

A. Write the dates. Use numbers.

Example: January twelfth January 12th

1. January third ______________________
2. February tenth ______________________
3. March seventeenth ______________________
4. April twenty-second ______________________

B. Write the dates. Use words.

Example: January 12th January twelfth

1. May 5th ______________________
2. June 11th ______________________
3. July 15th ______________________
4. August 31st ______________________

C. Look at this year's calendar. Answer the questions.

Example: When is New Year's Day? It's on January 1st.

1. When is Thanksgiving Day? ______________________
2. When is Valentine's Day? ______________________
3. When is the first day of summer? ______________________
4. When is Independence Day in the United States? ______________________
5. When is Labor day? ______________________

Name ______________________ Date ______________

Grammar

Use with student book page 126.

Simple Present: *have*

Subject	Verb *have*	Subject	Negative of *have*
I You We They	**have** a class today.	I You We They	**do not have** a class today. **don't have** a class today.
He She It	**has** a class today.	He She It	**does not have** a class today. **doesn't have** a class today.

A. Fill in the correct form of **have.**

Example: I ___have___ math class every day.

1. She ______________ art class today.
2. You ______________ basketball practice on Monday.
3. We ______________ the schedule.
4. They ______________ the textbook.
5. The teacher ______________ a computer and printer.

B. Correct the mistakes.

Example: I don't has science class on Friday, May 22nd.
I don't have science class on Friday, May 22nd.

1. Sam have an art show on June 30th.
____
2. Do we has class on June 10th?
____
3. We have don't a test on Tuesday.
____
4. He a football game Saturday, October 1st.
____

Name ______________________________ Date ______________

Grammar

Use with student book page 127.

Simple Present Tense

Simple Present Tense			
subject	simple present	subject	negative of simple present
I You We They	**read** every day.	I You We They	**do not read** every day. **don't read** every day.
He She It	**reads** every day.	He She It	**does not read** every day. **doesn't read** every day.

Note: Add **s** to the verb if it follows **he, she,** or **it.**

A. Read the sentences. Look at the subjects and verbs. Decide if the sentences are correct or not. Write correct if the sentence is correct. If it is not correct, write a correct sentence.

Example: Tim like science. Tim likes science.

1. Lin reads Chinese. ______________________________
2. Write e-mail every day. ______________________________
3. He does not speaks Spanish. ______________________________
4. She walks to school every Friday. ______________________________
5. We to music every night. ______________________________
6. My sister don't like to write letters. ______________________________

B. Write the correct form of the verb in parentheses ( ).

Example: They walk to the store on Fridays. (walk)

1. They ____________ late every Saturday. (sleep)
2. Min-ho ____________ his aunt on Sundays. (visit)
3. I ____________ to music as I ____________ the newspaper. (listen / read)
4. Ricardo ____________ to play baseball. (like)
5. You ____________ the question. (answer)

Name ______________________________ Date ________________

Grammar Expansion

Wh- Questions in Simple Present Tense

Wh- questions give information about **who, what, when, where, why,** and **how.**

Wh- Word	Asks About	Verb *be* (*Wh-* word + is + noun)	Other Verbs (*Wh-* word + do / does + subject + verb)
Who	a person	Who **is** she?	Who **do** you **work** for?
What	a thing	What **is** your name?	What **does** she **think?**
When	a time	When **is** the game?	When **do** classes **finish?**
Where	a place	Where **is** the dog?	Where **does** he **live?**
Why	a reason	Why **is** he tired?	Why **do** they **study** math?
How	a method	How **is** your mother?	How **does** he **feel?**

A. Match the question word with what it asks about.

Example: __c__ time — a. who

1. _____ place — b. what
2. _____ the way something was done — ~~c. when~~
3. _____ person — d. where
4. _____ thing — e. why
5. _____ reason — f. how

B. Write a **wh-** question with each word in parentheses ( ).

Example: (Why) Why is he home?
He's home because he doesn't have work.

1. (Who) ______________________________
Mary and Jan are in the school play.

2. (What) ______________________________
I have math class now.

3. (When) ______________________________
The football game is at 6:00.

4. (Where) ______________________________
The pep rally is in the gymnasium.

Name ______________________________ Date ________________

Word Study

Use with student book page 128.

/aw/ Sound in all, alk

A. Say the word for each picture. Circle the word for the picture.

Example:  wall (walk)

1.  call chalk

2.  call chalk

3.  balk ball

4.   walk wall

5.   talk tall

6.   wall walk

B. Write the missing letters.

Example: Now I am short but soon I will be t all.

1. I will c______ you on my cell phone.
2. The sidewalk is slippery, so don't f______ down.
3. You write on the board with ch______.
4. It's fun to shop at the m______.
5. Corn grows on a big st______.
6. We lined up quietly in the h______.

Name ______________________ Date ______________

Writing Assignment

Invitation

Use with student book page 129.

A. You want to have a birthday party. Answer the questions to help you write the invitation.

Example: What kind of party is it? a birthday party

1. What time does your party start? ______________________

2. What time does your party end? ______________________

3. Where is your party? ______________________

B. Write your invitation.

You're invited!

What: ______________________

Where: ______________________

____

____

When: ______________________

____

R.S.V.P.

(850) 555-3459

Name ______________________ Date ______________

Vocabulary From the Reading

Use with student book page 131.

Key Vocabulary

add	multiply
diagram	operation
divide	solve
equation	subtract

A. Match the Key Vocabulary word to the example.

Example: f add — a. 

1. _____ diagram — b. + − × ÷
2. _____ divide — c. ÷
3. _____ equation — d. ×
4. _____ multiply — e. 6 + 5 = 11
5. _____ subtract — ~~f. +~~
6. _____ solve — g. −
7. _____ operations — h. 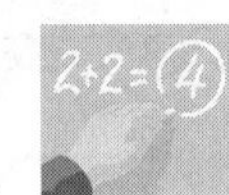

B. Use the correct Key Vocabulary word in each item. Use the list from Exercise A.

Example: You have six oranges and subtract four. Now you have two oranges.

1. When you ______________ $10 between two people, each person gets $5.
2. This problem is hard to ______________. I need help.
3. When you ______________ three by two, you get six.
4. Add, subtract, multiply, and divide are all ______________ in math.
5. You have $10 and ______________ $7—you now have $17.

Name ______________________ Date ______________

Reading Strategy

Set a Purpose for Reading

Use with student book page 132.

When you **set a purpose for reading,** you decide *why* you want to read something.

Academic Vocabulary for the Reading Strategy		
Word	**Explanation**	**Sample Sentence**
set	to decide or plan	Teachers **set** the class rules. They tell students what they need to do.
purpose	a reason for doing something	The **purpose** of a dictionary is to help you understand words you don't know.

A. Choose the correct answer. Write it on the line.

Example: You use the phone book to find a phone number.

find a phone number read for fun

1. You read your math notes many times to ______________________.

 do your homework study for a quiz

2. You read directions of this workbook to ______________________.

 find a phone number know how to do the exercises

3. You read the school newspaper to ______________________.

 know what is new at school study for a quiz

B. What is the author's purpose in writing these types of books?
Match the book to its purpose.

Example: e cookbook

1. ______ science textbook
2. ______ workbook
3. ______ dictionary
4. ______ storybook

a. for fun
b. to practice information from a textbook
c. to teach about science
d. to give the meaning of words
e. ~~to teach how to cook~~

Name ______________________ Date ______________

Text Genre

Textbook

Use with student book page 132.

Textbooks give information. Math textbooks have many features to help explain information.

Textbook	
explanations	tell you how to do something
examples	show you how to do something, and give you the answers
diagrams	pictures and charts that can help you understand something
exercises	math problems for you to solve

A. Match the textbook feature with the correct meaning.

Example: __d__ explanations

1. ______ examples
2. ______ diagrams
3. ______ exercises

a. show you how to do something and give you the answers
b. problems for you to solve
c. pictures and charts that can help you understand something
~~d. tell you how to do something~~

B. Write the correct textbook features below.

Example: You read about how to put paper into a printer. This is an __explanation__.

1. In a math book, you see: **2 + 2 =** ____. This is an ______________.
2. In a science book, you see a flower with its parts named. This is a ______________.
3. You read about how to start a computer. This is an ______________.
4. A picture is a ______________.
5. In a math book, you see: **2 + 3 = 5.** This is an ______________.
6. A graph or chart is a ______________.

Name ______________________ Date ______________

Reading Comprehension

Use with student book page 136.

A. Put the steps of a word problem in order.

Example: c	a. What do you need to do to this information? Add? Subtract? Multiply? Divide?
1. ______	b. Solve the equation.
2. ______	c. Read the word problem. Do you understand all the words?
3. ______	d. Write the problem as an equation.
4. ______	e. What information can you find in the word problem?
5. ______	f. What is the question? What do you need to find?

B. Answer the questions.

Example: What is a word problem?

A word problem uses words to tell you the problem.

1. Write a word problem.

____

____

2. Now solve your word problem. Use a diagram.

Name ______________________________ Date ______________

Text Elements

Graphs and Charts

Use with student book page 137.

Graphs and charts can give different information about the same numbers.

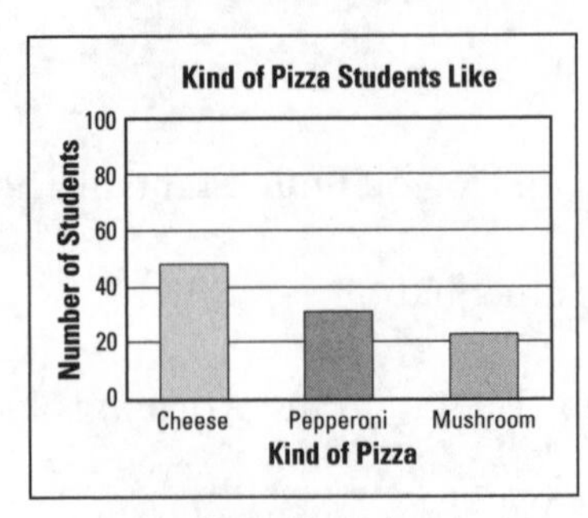

Bar Graph

Kind of Pizza Students Like

Mushroom 21%

Cheese 48%

Pepperoni 31%

Pie Chart

A. Answer the questions about the chart and graph above.

Example: What do graphs and charts do? They give information about numbers.

1. What is a pie chart used for? ______________________________

____

2. What is a bar graph used for? ______________________________

____

B. How much time do you spend doing these activities?

Do homework: ______________ Eat dinner: ______________

Talk on the phone: ______________ Be with friends: ______________

C. Look at Sara's information on the right. Then make a bar graph of how much time you spend on each activity above. Use your answers from exercise B.

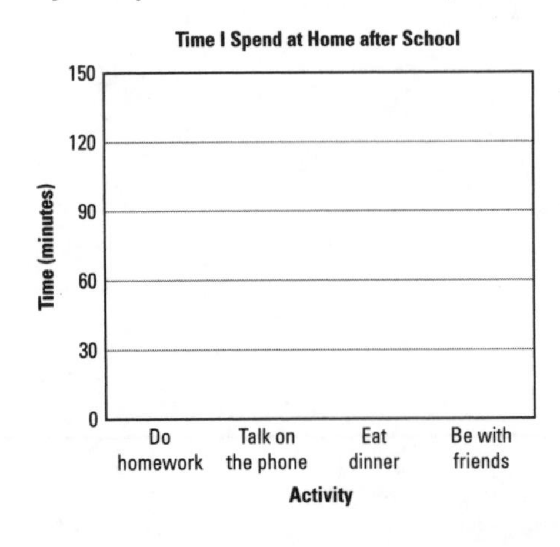

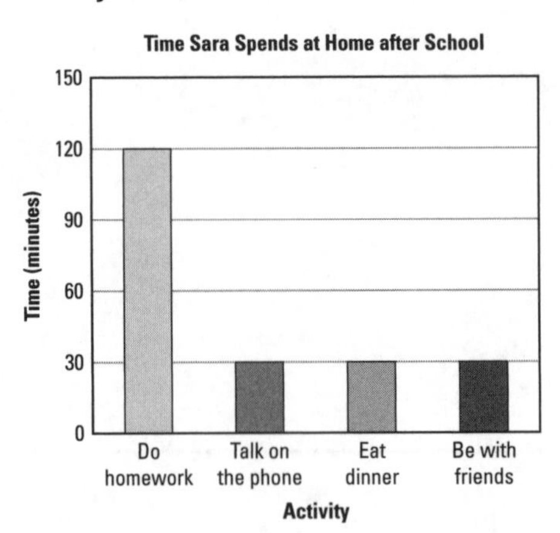

Name ______________________ Date ______________

Vocabulary

Describing People's Appearance

Use with student book pages 152–153.

curly	short
dark	shoulder-length
light	straight
long	

A. Circle the words in parentheses ( ) that describe people.

Example: She has (short / shoulder-length / long), (curly / straight) hair.

Describe the girl. Circle the words.

1. She has (short / shoulder-length / long), (curly / straight) hair.

Describe the boy. Circle the words.

2. He has (short / shoulder-length / long), (curly / straight) hair.
3. His hair color is (light / dark).

B. Now write two sentences about your hair.

Example: I have shoulder-length, curly hair. My hair color is dark brown.

____

____

C. Now write two sentences about a classmate.

Example: Rebecca has short, curly hair. Her hair color is dark red.

____

____

Name ______________________ Date ______________

Vocabulary

More Ways to Describe People's Appearance

Use with student book pages 154–155.

Complete the conversations.

Conversation #1

Antonio: Do you know Ken?

Jasmine: I'm not sure. What does he look like?

Antonio: He has short, dark brown, curly **(example)** ____hair____ and green (1) ______________.

Jasmine: Does he wear glasses?

Antonio: (2) Yes, ______________.

Conversation #2

Ming: Do (3) ______________ Jessica?

Tomas: I'm (4) ______________. What does she look like?

Ming: She (5) ______________ blond hair. She (6) ______________ blue eyes.

Tomas: (7) ______________ glasses?

Ming: (8) No, ______________.

Conversation #3

Trung: Do (9) ______________ Mary?

Karen: I'm not sure. What does she (10) ______________?

Trung: Her (11) ______________ is red. She has blue eyes and wears (12) ______________.

Karen: Yes, I do know her!

Name ______________________________ Date ____________________

Grammar

Use with student book page 156.

Simple Past Tense: Regular and Irregular Verbs

Regular Verb	Simple Past Tense	Affirmative Statement
want	want**ed**	They **wanted** pizza on Saturday.
dance	danc**ed**	Maria **danced** to music last night.
play	play**ed**	We **played** baseball yesterday.

Irregular Verb	Simple Past Tense	Affirmative Statement
have	**had**	He **had** his keys in his pocket.
go	**went**	We **went** to a movie yesterday.
do	**did**	They **did** their homework before class.
make	**made**	I **made** breakfast at 7:00.

A. Complete each sentence with the past tense form of the regular verb in parentheses.

Example: I ____walked____ to school yesterday. (walk)

1. We ____________________ together at the school dance. (dance)
2. They ____________________ to go with us to the store. (want)
3. The class ____________________ basketball in the gym. (play)
4. Ana ____________________ to music in her room. (listen)
5. Sandra's brother ____________________ the dishes after lunch. (wash)

B. Complete each sentence with the past tense form of the irregular verb in parentheses.

Example: He ____had____ his keys in his pocket. (have)

1. We ____________________ no milk. (have)
2. She ____________________ to the doctor on Tuesday. (go)
3. The class ____________________ very well on the test. (do)
4. My mother ____________________ a chocolate cake for my birthday. (make)
5. My sister ____________________ to Mexico last summer. (go)

Name ______________________ Date ______________

Grammar

Use with student book page 157.

Simple Past Tense: Negative Statements and *Be*

Affirmative Statement	Negative Statement
Celia **listened** to music.	Celia **didn't listen** to music.
We **went** to the concert.	We **didn't go** to the concert.

Affirmative Statement	Negative Statement
I **was** here.	I **wasn't** here.
You **were** right.	You **weren't** right.
He / She / It **was** late.	He / She / It **wasn't** late.
We **were** happy.	We **weren't** happy.
They **were** on time.	They **weren't** on time.

A. Change the affirmative statements to negative statements.

Example: Celia listened to music. Celia didn't listen to music.

1. We went to the concert. ______________________
2. Amanda danced at the school dance. ______________________
3. He went to the football game. ______________________
4. They played this game. ______________________

B. Are the negative statements correct? Write each sentence correctly. If it is correct, write **correct.**

Example: Celia not listen to music. Celia did not listen to music.

1. I didn't have the keys. ______________________
2. His mother not make a chocolate cake. ______________________
3. We didn't need the rulers. ______________________
4. She didn't the dishes. ______________________
5. Lu didn't listened to music. ______________________
6. They not played last Saturday. ______________________

Name ______________________ Date ______________

Grammar Expansion

Wh- Questions in Simple Past Tense

Verb *be* (*Wh-* word + was or were + noun)	Other Verbs (*Wh-* word + did + subject + verb)
Who **was** she?	Who **did** you **work** for?
What **were** your classes like last year?	What **did** I **think?**
When **was** the game?	When **did** classes **end?**
Where **were** the dogs?	Where **did** he **live?**
Why **was** I tired?	Why **did** they **go** there?
How **was** the banana?	How **did** it **fit?**

A. Complete each sentence. Use the correct word in parentheses.

Example: Who __was__ she? (was / did)

1. When __________ the music stop? (was / did)
2. What __________ the color of her shirt? (did / was)
3. Where __________ the cat sleep last night? (did / were)
4. Why __________ you in the store so late? (was / were)
5. How __________ the students in the school concert? (was / were)

B. Complete each sentence. Write the past tense form of the verb in parentheses.

Example: What __did__ she say? (do)

1. Who __________ the students that left? (be)
2. When __________ we go to sleep last night? (do)
3. Where __________ they go after the party? (do)
4. Why __________ he so happy? (be)
5. How __________ you get to school today? (do)

Name ______________________ Date ______________

Word Study

Use with student book pages 158–159.

Initial Blends: br, cr, fr, gr, pr, dr, tr

A. Say the word for the picture. Circle the word that starts with the same sound.

Example: (crop) drip tram great

1. fresh brick grin prom
2. trim free trap swam
3. brim prune frog gram
4. grape brush front prince
5. prop drag tree group
6. green price trip friend
7. 20 trail gram brag twins

B. Divide the words into beginning, middle, and end sounds. Keep blends together.

Examples: a. crab cr / a / b b. brand br / a / nd

1. truck ______ 3. print ______ 5. twin ______

2. swan ______ 4. frog ______ 6. cramp ______

Name ________________________ Date ________________

Word Study

Common Irregular Past Tense Verbs

Use with student book page 160.

A. Read the verb. Circle the common irregular past tense of each verb.

Example: hit hitted hits (hit)

1. cut cutted cuts cut
2. run ran runned ranned
3. leave leaved left leaving
4. say said sayed says
5. buy buyed buy bought

B. Write the common irregular past tense of the verb in each sentence.

Example: sit My dog ____sat____ down.

1. keep She ________________ the gift from her friend.
2. pay I ________________ ten dollars for my new books.
3. think Carmen ________________ about her grandmother often.
4. let Our teacher ________________ us play outside yesterday.
5. get Sam ________________ a new bike for his birthday.

C. Read each sentence. Circle the correct form of the irregular past tense of each verb.

Example: Mom ((put)/ putted) the box on the shelf.

1. My grandfather (comed / came) to school with me.
2. He (told / telled) the class about his life in Japan.
3. My classmates (thought / thinks) his story was interesting.
4. Our teacher (says / said) he should come again.
5. I (feeled / felt) so proud of my grandfather!
6. Each boy (payed / paid) for his movie ticket.
7. I (get / got) an M3P player for my birthday.
8. We (boughted / bought) some sandwiches for lunch.

Name ______________________ Date ______________

Writing Assignment

Narrative Paragraph

Use with student book page 161.

Parts of a Paragraph

A. Match each paragraph part with its meaning.

Example: d paragraph

1. _____ topic sentence
2. _____ indent
3. _____ supporting sentences

a. leave space at the beginning of the paragraph

b. first sentence that tells what the paragraph is about

c. sentences that give facts and details about the topic

~~d. a group of sentences about one main idea~~

Paragraph Preparation

B. Make a list of what you did last weekend.

Example: I slept late Saturday morning.

1. ______________________
2. ______________________
3. ______________________
4. ______________________

C. Outlines help organize ideas. Complete the outline below with the information above.

A. On Saturday

Example: I slept late in the morning.

1. ______________________
2. ______________________

B. On Sunday

1. ______________________
2. ______________________

Name ______________________ Date ______________

Vocabulary From the Reading

Use with student book page 163.

aunt	**son**
cousin	**uncle**
daughter	

A. Match each Key Vocabulary word with its meaning.

Example: __e__ aunt — a. male child

1. _____ cousin — b. aunt and uncle's child
2. _____ daughter — c. parent's brother
3. _____ son — d. female child
4. _____ uncle — ~~e. parent's sister~~

B. Complete the sentences with the correct Key Vocabulary word.

Example: Sandra is Manuela and Jorge's __daughter__.

1. Pablo is Alicia's ______________.
2. Alicia and Paul are Maria's ______________.
3. Paul is Saul's ______________.

Name ______________________________ Date ________________

Reading Strategy

Use with student book page 164.

Understand the Author's Message

Usually an author sends a message. This message is the meaning of the story.

Word	Explanation	Sample Sentence
author	someone who writes something, like a story or a poem	The **author** wrote three books.
message	piece of information someone is trying to give or communicate to someone else	There was a **message** in the bottle.

A. Circle the letters of the answers.

Example: What does an author do?

a. reads a message (b.) sends a message

1. Where do you find the message?

   a. in a special paragraph b. in the characters' actions

2. Why is there a message?

   a to teach the readers b. to learn from the readers

3. Why do we look for a message?

   a. to learn from the author b. to play a game

The Boy Who Cried "Wolf"
by Aesop

There was a boy who lived in a small town. One day the boy was bored. He said, "I saw a wolf! I saw a wolf!" The farmers were scared. They ran to the boy, but there was no wolf. The boy thought this was fun. The next day, he did it again. The farmers came again, but there was no wolf. The boy laughed. Later, a wolf came. The boy told the farmers about the wolf. No one believed him.

B. Read the story. Then circle the letter of the answers to the questions.

Example: Who is the author of "The Boy Who Cried 'Wolf'"?

a. a boy (b.) Aesop c. a farmer

1. Why did the boy say he saw a wolf?

   a. He was happy. b. He was scared. c. He was bored.

2. How did the farmers feel when they saw there was no wolf?

   a. They were scared. b. They were angry. c. They thought the boy was funny.

3. Why didn't the farmers come later when there was a wolf?

   a. They didn't believe the boy. b. They were bored. c. They were happy.

Name ______________________ Date ______________

Text Genre

Use with student book page 164.

Poetry

A poem is a piece of **poetry.** There are different kinds of poems. Some use words that **rhyme** at the end of each line like **cat/mat** and **bun/one.** Free verse poems do not rhyme. The author of a poem is a poet.

Poetry	
rhyme	words that sound alike at the end
free verse	poems that don't rhyme
stanza	a group of lines in a poem

A. Complete each sentence. Use the correct word in parentheses.

Example: A ___poet___ is a person who writes poetry. (poem / poet / poetry)

1. A piece of poetry is called a ____________. (poem / poet / poetry)
2. Free verse is a way to describe a ____________. (poem / poet / poetry)
3. A poem with words that sound alike at the end of each line is a poem that ____________. (free verse / rhymes / stanza)
4. A ____________ is like a paragraph in a poem. (free verse / rhymes / stanza)

B. Read the poem. Then answer the questions.

Twinkle*, Twinkle, Little Star

Twinkle, twinkle, little star,
How I wonder what you are
Up above the world so high
Like a diamond in the sky.

Twinkle, twinkle, little star,
How I wonder what you are.

*__Twinkle__ means to shine lightly.

Example: Write the first two words that rhyme in the poem. ___star/are___

1. Write the second two words that rhyme in the poem. ____________
2. How many lines are in the first stanza of the poem? ____________
3. How many lines are in the second stanza of the poem? ____________
4. How are free verse and poems that rhyme different? ____________

Name ______________________ Date ______________

Reading Comprehension

Use with student book page 168.

A. Answer the questions about the poem on page 166.

Example: __c__ What is the title of the poem?

a. Some people b. one thing is love c. What Is a Family?

1. _____ Which word rhymes with **mother** in Stanza 1?

a. father b. daughter c. brother

2. _____ Which word rhymes with **away** in Stanza 4?

a. family b. people c. day

3. _____ What is the message of the poem?

a. Each family is different b. Love is not important c. Uncles live far away

B. Answer the questions about the poem on page 167.

Example: __a__ What is the title of the poem?

a. Our Grandmother b. Grandma c. We love her

1. _____ What does grandma do in the poem?

a. She plays video games b. She tells funny jokes c. She has red hair

2. _____ What kind of poem is it?

a. It is a rhyming poem b. It is a free verse poem c. It is not a poem

3. _____ What is the message of the poem?

a. Grandma likes baseball b. Grandma wears perfume c. Grandma loves us

C. Answer the questions. Compare and contrast the poems.

Example: Contrast. Which poem has a shape? Our Grandmother

1. Compare. How are the two poems similar?

____

____

2. Contrast. How are the two poems different?

____

____

____

Name ______________________ Date ______________

Literary Elements

Use with student book page 169.

Repetition and Alliteration

Repetition is saying or repeating the same word, or words, again and again.
Alliteration is repeating the same consonant.

A. Circle **repetition** when the sentence has repetition. Circle **alliteration** when the sentence has alliteration.

Example: She sells seashells by the sea shore. **repetition** **(alliteration)**

1. Peter Piper picked a peck of pickled peppers. **repetition** **alliteration**
2. I have a dream, I have a dream. **repetition** **alliteration**
3. I am very, very, very, very tired. **repetition** **alliteration**
4. The sun set slowly on the silvery sea. **repetition** **alliteration**
5. We wanted to walk on a wet windy day. **repetition** **alliteration**

B. Underline all of the alliterated sounds.

Example: Peter Piper picked a peck of pickled peppers.

1. Susan sank slowly into the soft, satin sofa on Sunday.
2. The boy bounced the brown ball on the boardwalk.
3. Candice can come to the concert with us.
4. Did the dirty dog dig up all of the dirt in the driveway?

C. Make two sentences that use repetition.

Example: "I love you," my mother says. "I love you, I love you, I love you."

1. ______________________

2. ______________________

D. Now, make two sentences that use alliteration. Use the sounds given.

Example: (R) Ralph really likes to run on rough roads in the rain.

1. (L) ______________________

2. (B) ______________________

Name ______________________ Date ______________

Writing Conventions

Use with student book page 169.

Spelling: Commonly Confused Homophones

Homophones	Sentence
you're = you are	**You're** a teacher.
your = possessive adjective	**Your** bag is blue.
it's = it is	**It's** two o'clock.
its = possessive adjective	The desk is broken. **Its** leg is broken.
they're = they are	**They're** students.
their = possessive adjective	**Their** parents are happy.
there = place	Put your bag over **there**.

A. Circle the correct word.

Example: That's not (you're / your) pen.

1. What's (you're / your) name?
2. You can leave when (it's / its) four o'clock.
3. That is (they're / their / there) red car.
4. (They're / Their / There) house is over (they're / their / there).
5. (You're / Your) right!
6. (It's / Its) lid fell on the floor.
7. I think (they're / their / there) on the desk.

B. Complete the sentences. Write the correct word.

Example: I think ___it's___ in the wrong place.

1. He knows ______________ right. (your / you're)
2. ______________ it is! (Their / They're / There)
3. ______________ coat is so shiny. (It's / Its)
4. ______________ in the classroom. (Their / They're / There)
5. We don't know where ______________ cat is. (your / you're)

Name ______________________ Date ______________

Vocabulary

Everyday Activities

Use with student book pages 174–175.

eat breakfast	leave for school
get up	get home
get dressed	do your homework
get ready for school	go to bed

A. Put the activities in the correct order.

do my homework	get dressed	get home
get up	go to bed	leave for school

Example: First, I get up. Fourth, I ______.

Second, I ______. Fifth, I ______.

Third, I ______. Sixth, I ______.

B. Tell the time. Use numbers.

Example: It's 6:15. 1. It's ______. 2. It's ______.

C. Tell the time. Use words.

Example: It's eight fifteen 1. It's ______.

2. It's ______. 3. It's ______.

Name ______________________ Date ______________

Vocabulary

Home Activities

Use with student book pages 176–177.

A. Look at the pictures. Complete the sentences.

Example: Can you play football now?
I cannot. I have to write a report.

1. What do you do on Wednesday afternoons?
I ______________ on Wednesday afternoons.

2. Can you play now?
I cannot. I have to ______________.

3. What do you do after each meal?
I ______________.

B. Here is a list of things you did last weekend. You were very busy. Use a verb to complete the sentences. Use the past tense.

Example: I cleaned my room.

1. On Saturday morning, I ______________ the dishes after breakfast.
2. Then I ______________ a report.
3. I took a nap. After that, I ______________ to music.
4. On Sunday morning, I ______________ for the science test.
5. In the afternoon, I ______________ for the school concert.
6. And I ______________ for a spelling test.

Name ______________________ Date ______________

Grammar

Use with student book page 178.

Yes/No Questions and Short Answers: *be* and Simple Present

Yes/No Questions and Short Answers: *be*			
statements	*yes/no* questions	short answers	
He **is** late.	**Is** he late?	Yes, he **is**.	No, he **isn't**.
They **are** here.	**Are** they here?	Yes, they **are**.	No, they **aren't**.
He **was** late.	**Was** he late?	Yes, he **was**.	No, he **wasn't**.
They **were** here.	**Were** they here?	Yes, they **were**.	No, they **weren't**.

Yes/No Questions and Short Answers: Simple Present			
statements	*yes/no* questions	short answers	
He **eats** lunch.	**Does** he **eat** lunch?	Yes, he **does**.	No, he **doesn't**.
They **study** hard.	**Do** they **study** hard?	Yes, they **do**.	No, they **don't**.

A. Circle the correct word.

Example: ((Is) / Were) your sister ready for school?

1. (Are / Is) they in school now?
2. (Was / Were) he at home?
3. (Are / Is) she in the car?
4. (Was / Were) he at the party?

B. Rewrite the first two questions from Exercise A on the lines below. Then answer the questions with **yes.**

Example: Is your sister ready for school? Yes, she is.

1. ______________________________

2. ______________________________

Rewrite the last two questions from Exercise A on the lines below. Then answer the questions with **no.**

Example: Is your sister ready for school? No, she isn't.

3. ______________________________

4. ______________________________

Name ______________________ Date ______________

Grammar

Use with student book page 179.

Yes / No Questions and Short Answers: Simple Past

Yes/No Questions and Short Answers: Simple Past			
statements	*yes/no* questions	short answers	
He **ate** lunch.	**Did** he **eat** lunch?	Yes, he **did**.	No, he **didn't**.
They **studied**.	**Did** they **study**?	Yes, they **did**.	No, they **didn't**.

A. Read each sentence. Then write a question in the simple past.

Example: He ate breakfast. Did he eat breakfast?

1. They studied. ______________________
2. She practiced music. ______________________
3. I washed the dishes. ______________________
4. We tried to clean the room. ______________________

B. Answer the questions. Write **Yes, I did** or **No, I didn't.**

Example: Did you study on Saturday? Yes, I did.

1. I ate breakfast today. Did you eat breakfast today? ______________
2. I did my homework yesterday. Did you do your homework yesterday? ______
3. I didn't clean my room today. Did you clean your room today? __________
4. I washed dishes yesterday. Did you wash dishes yesterday? __________

C. Write the past tense of the verb in parentheses. Be careful to spell the verbs correctly.

Example: I ______tried______ to sleep on the couch. (try)

1. He ______________ for the biology test. (study)
2. We ______________ when they got ______________. (cry / marry)
3. The class ______________ to catch the bus to the art show. (hurry)

Name ______________________ Date ______________

Grammar Expansion

Simple Past Tense: Irregular Verbs

Some verbs have an irregular form in the simple past tense.

Irregular Verbs	
Simple Present	**Simple Past**
I **write** letters every week.	I **wrote** letters every week.
You **get** home at 7:00.	You **got** home at 7:00.
She **leaves** work at 5:00.	She **left** work at 5:00.
We **do** our homework.	We **did** our homework.
They **go** to school.	They **went** to school.
I **eat** cheese pizza.	I **ate** cheese pizza.

A. Put the verbs in parentheses ( ) in the past tense.

Example: I ___did___ my math homework yesterday. (do)

1. We ______________ a letter to my aunt. (write)
2. Adrian ______________ home at 7:45 yesterday morning. (leave)
3. I ______________ cheese pizza last night. (eat)
4. The teacher ______________ birthday cards this morning. (get)
5. You ______________ the last banana. (eat)
6. My father and sister ______________ to the store on Sunday. (go)

B. Make your own sentences. Use the verbs in parentheses ( ), but change them into the past tense.

Example: (eat) I ate a sandwich and some carrots.

1. (write) ______________________________
2. (do) ______________________________
3. (go) ______________________________
4. (leave) ______________________________

Name ______________________ Date ______________

Word Study

Use with student book page 180.

Blends: st, sn, sp, sc, sl, sm, sk

A. Draw a line from the picture to the word.

1. star  a. 

2. snow b. 

3. spoon c. 

4. scarf d. 

5. sled e. 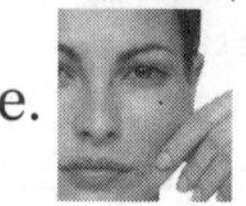

6. smile f. 

7. skin g. 

B. Unscramble the letters to match the picture.

Example:  p c e s a ___space___

1. k n s i ______________

2. c r f s a ______________

3. s i m e l ______________

4. 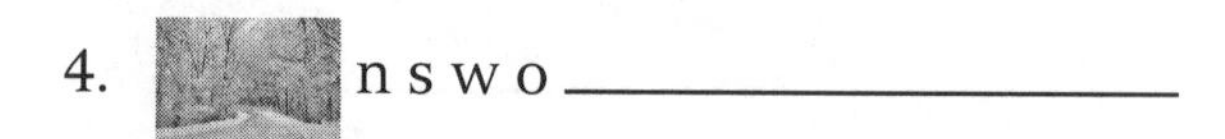 n s w o ______________

5. t r s a ______________

6. s e l d ______________

Name ________________________ Date ______________

Writing Assignment

Diary Entry

Use with student book page 181.

A. Think about something interesting, funny, or exciting that happened to you today, this week, or last weekend. Answer the questions.

1. What topic do you want to write about?

____

2. When did it happen?

____

3. Who was there?

____

4. Where did it happen?

____

5. How did you feel when it happened?

____

B. Now put your topic in the middle square. Then put your information in the other squares.

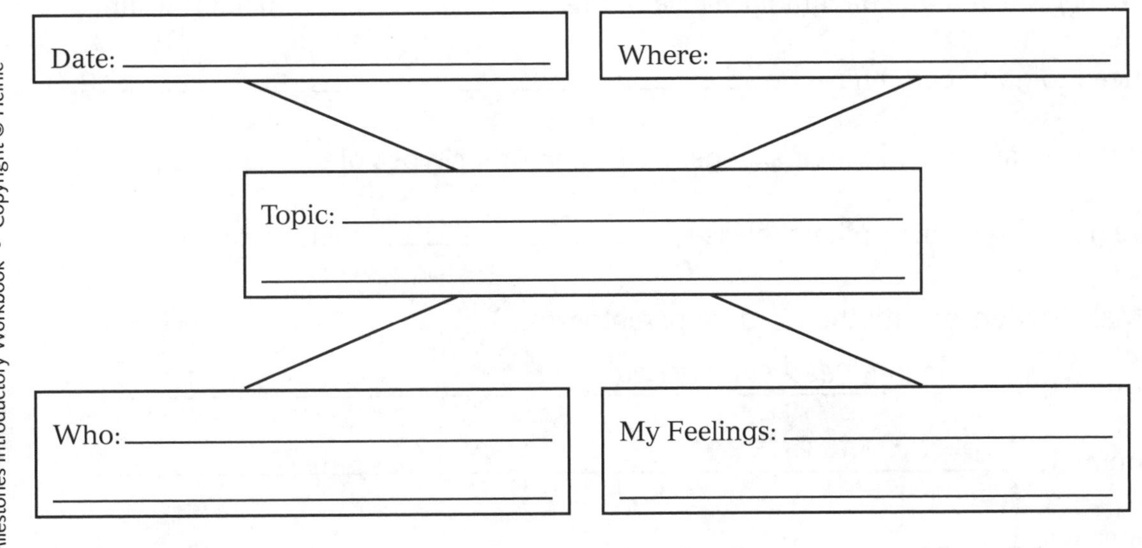

Name ______________________ Date ______________

Vocabulary From the Reading

Use with student book page 183.

Key Vocabulary

animal	heat	plant
energy	organism	transfer

A. Match the words.

Example: d transfer — a. warmth

1. ____ animal — b. cat
2. ____ energy — c. animal or plant
3. ____ heat — ~~d. move~~
4. ____ organism — e. flower
5. ____ plant — f. power

B. Complete each sentence. Use the correct Key Vocabulary word.

Example: An organism is a name for an animal or a plant.

1. A tree is a kind of ______________________.
2. We feel warm in the daytime because of the ______________ from the sun.
3. I need to go to bed; I have no ______________________.
4. At the pet store, we saw cats, dogs, birds, and other types of ______________.
5. We must move these plants; please ______________ them to that table.

C. Make sentences with the words in parentheses ( ).

Example: (plant) Plants need sun and water.

1. (animal) ______________________
2. (energy) ______________________
3. (transfer) ______________________

Name ______________________ Date ______________

Reading Strategy

Use with student book page 184.

Use Context to Find Meaning

When you don't know the meaning of a new word or sentence, look at the words around it.

Word	Explanation	Sample Sentence
context	the information around a word or phrase	You can understand a word by seeing it in context.
meaning	a definition or an explanation	Dictionaries can help you find the meaning of a word you don't know.

A. Find the meaning of the bold words. Underline the words that help find meaning.

Example: Green plants make, or produce their own food. Plants are **producers**.

1. In **photosynthesis,** plants change energy in sunlight to energy in food.
2. **Consumers** eat plants and other animals to get energy.
3. Animals that eat other animals are called **carnivores**.
4. In a **food chain,** one organism eats another for energy.

B. Use the context to find the meaning of the words in bold. Write the meaning on the line.

Example: I like running, jumping, and **tumbling.** Tumbling is a type of exercise or moving.

1. The dog, the cat, and the **parrot** are in the house.

____

____

2. I draw a circle, a square, and an **oval.**

____

____

3. In my school we can play football, basketball, and **lacrosse.**

____

____

Name ______________________________ Date ______________

Text Genre

Use with student book page 184.

Informational Text: Magazine Article with Diagrams

A magazine article is a short work of nonfiction. People usually read magazine articles for information and enjoyment.

Magazine Article	
diagrams or illustrations	pictures and charts that can help you understand
captions	explanations of the illustrations
headings	what each section is about

Read the article. Then answer the questions.

Wildlife Cycles

by Kristy Perry

The sun is a powerful source of energy. Its energy feeds the Earth's plants. As the plants grow, they give off heat. Grass and plants transfer sunlight into energy for food. Then, a grasshopper eats grass for energy. A bird eats grasshoppers for energy. A wolf eats birds for energy. All organisms need energy.

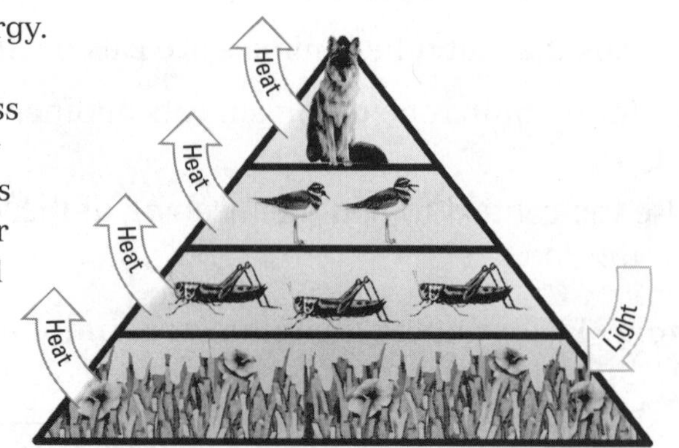

Energy Pyramid

Now answer the questions.

Example: Who is the author of this article? Kristy Perry

1. What does the heading of this article say? ______________

2. What kind of diagram is in this article? ______________

3. What does the caption of the diagram say? ______________

Name ______________________ Date ______________

Reading Comprehension

Use with student book page 188.

A. Identify the roles of organisms in a food chain.

Example: What does the grasshopper eat? The grasshopper eats the grass.

1. What does the frog eat?

____

2. What does the snake eat?

____

3. What do producers do?

____

4. What do consumers do?

____

5. What do herbivores do?

____

6. What do carnivores do?

____

7. What do decomposers do?

____

B. In your own words, describe what happens in an energy pyramid.

____

____

____

____

____

Name ______________________ Date ______________

Text Element

Use with student book page 189.

Glossary

A glossary is an alphabetical list of words and definitions in the back of a textbook.

This is an example of a glossary.

caption (kap'shən) *n.* explains the information in a photograph, illustration, or chart
cast of characters (kast ov kar'ik tərz) *n.* the people in a play
cause (kŏz) *n.* a reason why something happens
character (kar'ik tər) *n.* person in a story, may be imaginary or a real person
cloudy (klou' dē) *adj.* describes weather when there are many clouds in the sky
conversation (kon vər sā' shən) *n.* when people talk to one another

A. Write the definitions of the words.

Example: cast of characters: the people in a play

1. cloudy: ______________________
2. cause: ______________________
3. conversation: ______________________

B. Answer the questions about the glossary above.

Example: What makes it easy to see the vocabulary words in a glossary?
The words are bold.

1. What do the letters in parentheses ( ) teach you?
____
2. What does *"n."* mean?
____
3. What does *"adj."* mean?
____
4. What is another word for **definition?**
____

Name ______________________ Date ______________

Vocabulary

After-school Activities

Use with student book pages 204–205.

check my e-mail	**listen to music**	**ride my bike**
clean my room	**meet my friends**	**watch TV**
do my homework	**play basketball**	

A. Write the vocabulary words below the after-school activities.

Example: meet my friends

1. ______________

2. ______________

3. ______________

4. ______________

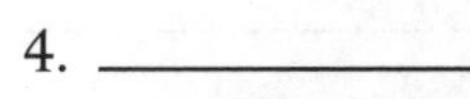

5. ______________

6. ______________

B. Complete the sentences.

Karen: What do you do after school, Max?

Max: I always check my **(example)** e-mail.

Karen: I always (1) ______________ my homework first. Then sometimes I eat a snack and (2) ______________ TV.

Karen: I usually meet my (3) ______________ after I do my homework.

Max: After I relax, I always do my homework. I often play (4) ______________ or (5) ______________ my bike.

Karen: When I am back home, I usually (6) ______________ my e-mail.

Name ______________________ Date ______________

Vocabulary

Weather

Use with student book pages 206–207.

cloudy	snowing	cold	nice
raining	sunny	hot	terrible

A. Write a sentence about the weather in each picture.

Example: It's sunny.

1. ______________

2. ______________

3. ______________

B. Complete the sentences.

Dante: Hi, Ana! What's the weather like today in Arizona?

Ana: The weather is **(example)** nice. It's hot and (1) ______________.

Dante: In Colorado, the weather isn't very warm. It's (2) ______________.

Ana: Is it (3) ______________?

Dante: No, it's too cold for rain. It's (4) ______________.

C. Write sentences about the weather in your town today.

____

____

Name ______________________________ Date ____________________

Grammar

Use with student book page 208.

Present Continuous Tense

The present continuous tense tells about an action that is happening right now.

Present Continuous Statements		
subject pronoun	**be**	**verb ending in *-ing***
I	**am**	talk**ing**.
He / She / It	**is**	
We / You / They	**are**	

A. Complete each sentence with the present continuous form of the verb in parentheses.

Example: It's hot outside. We ___are swimming___ in the pool. (swim)

1. I ____________________ my bike. (ride)
2. You ____________________ for a gift. (shop)
3. He ____________________ to the store. (go)
4. They ____________________ their e-mail. (check)
5. We ____________________ basketball. (play)

B. Write sentences about the pictures in the present continuous tense.

Example: ___They are meeting with friends.___

1. ______________________________

2. ______________________________

3. ______________________________

Name ______________________ Date ______________

Grammar

Use with student book page 209.

Present Continuous Questions and Negative Statements

Present Continuous Questions
Am I **going** with you?
Is he **walking** to the bus stop?
What **are** you **doing**?
Where **is** he **going**?

Present Continuous Negative Statements
Put **not** between the form of **be** and the verb ending in **ing**.
I **am not walking** to the mall.

A. Change the statements into questions.

Example: I am going with you. Am I going with you?

1. He is walking home. ______________________
2. They are riding their bikes. ______________________
3. You are writing a letter. ______________________
4. She is moving after school ends. ______________________

B. Now answer the questions above using negative statements.

Example: Am I going with you? No, I am not going with you.

1. ______________________
2. ______________________
3. ______________________
4. ______________________

C. Put the words in the correct order.

Example: (you? / going / I / with / Am) Am I going with you?

1. (school. / is / to / going / not / He) ______________________
2. (Are / you / your / doing / homework?) ______________________
3. (for / my / shopping / mother. / am / I) ______________________

____

4. (in / are / seat. / You / my / sitting) ______________________

Name ______________________ Date ______________

Grammar Expansion

Wh- Questions in the Present Continuous Tense

Look at the chart below to see how to ask a question about what someone is doing right now.

Wh- Word	*Be*	Subject	*-ing* Verb
Who	are	you	calling?
What	is	he	thinking?
Where	is	she	living?
Why	are	they	going?
How	is	it	doing?

A. Write the correct form of the verb *be* and each verb in parentheses.

Example: Who ___are___ you ___calling___? (call)

1. Where ______________ the students ______________? (sit)
2. How ______________ they ______________? (play)
3. Why ______________ the driver ______________? (stop)

B. Write each question correctly. If it is correct, write **correct.**

Example: Where the students are sitting? ___Where are the students sitting?___

1. Who she helping is? ______________
2. Why are you running? ______________
3. Where is he ride his bike? ______________
4. How are the students doing? ______________

C. Make questions in the present continuous with the words in parentheses.

Example: (what / you / do / here) ___What are you doing here?___

1. (why / she / go) ______________
2. (where / he / go / to) ______________

Name ______________________________ Date ______________________

Word Study

Use with student book pages 210–211.

Beginning Blends: bl, cl, fl, sl, pl, gl
Consonant Clusters: squ, spr, str, scr, spl

A. Say the word for the picture. Circle the word for the picture.

Example: 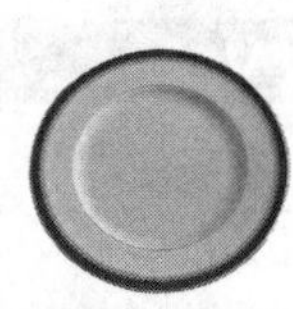 slate (plate)

1.  spray clay

3.  flare square

2.  globe strobe

4. 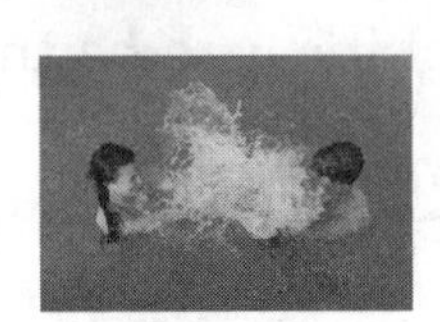 clash splash

B. Divide the words into beginning, middle, and end sounds. Keep blends together.

Example: clip cl / i / p

1. glad ____________
3. flat ____________
5. scrub ____________
2. split ____________
4. clap ____________
6. squid ____________

C. Read each word. Look at the picture. Change the word to match the picture.

Example: 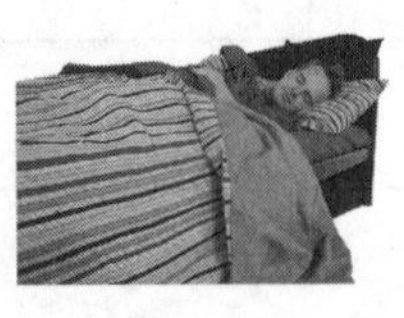 bleep sleep

1. 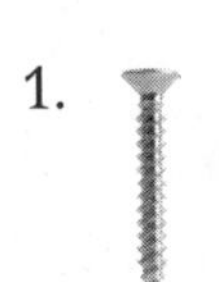 flew ____________

2.   slip ____________

Name ______________________________ Date ____________________

Word Study

Use with student book page 212.

Prefixes: un, dis, non, im

A. Match the prefix with the correct root word. Then write the root word with the prefix.

Example: unfair un   a. mature

1. ____________ dis   b. stop
2. ____________ non   c. like
3. ____________ im   d. fair

B. Read each sentence. Use a prefix to complete each underlined word.

Example: Lara was un happy with her dress.

1. She ____ liked the red fabric.
2. The stitches looked ____ perfect to her.
3. She was ____ happy with it.
4. She worked ____ stop to fix it.

C. Make words with each prefix. Use the words from the box below. One word can be used with more than one prefix.

agree	fair	fat	fiction	friendly	happy	like
perfect	possible	stop	trust	slip	polite	

un	dis	non	im
unhappy			

Name ____________________ Date ____________

Writing Assignment

Use with student book page 213.

A Descriptive Paragraph

Lorena Cabaltera

Friday in the Park

It is four o'clock on Friday afternoon. It is a beautiful day here in Tampa. I am sitting on a bench in Sunshine park. Many of my friends are in the park, too. Paulo is riding his bike. Nora and Donna are eating ice cream. Manny is listineing to music. What am I doing? I am doing my homework. I am writing a paragraph for my English class!

A. Make a list of five people. Then write what each person is doing right now.

Name	Activity
Example: Janet	checking her e-mail
1.	
2.	
3.	
4.	
5.	

B. Now write sentences in the present continuous. Use the information in your chart.

Example: Janet is checking her e-mail.

1. ____________________

2. ____________________

3. ____________________

4. ____________________

5. ____________________

Name ______________________ Date ______________

Vocabulary From the Reading

Use with student book page 215.

Key Vocabulary

fall off	late
gate	run
holiday	watch

A. Match each Key Vocabulary word with its definition.

Example: c fall off

1. ______ gate
2. ______ holiday
3. ______ late
4. ______ run
5. ______ watch

a. special day
b. after a time
~~c. move to a lower place~~
d. small clock
e. door in a fence or a wall
f. move your legs quickly

B. Fill in each blank. Choose the correct word in parentheses ( ).

Example: My watch stopped. I don't know the time. (watch / gate)

1. We can go into the park. The ______________ is open. (watch / gate)
2. It's 9:15, and the train comes at 9:10. I'm ______________. (watch / late)
3. Be careful not to ______________ your bike. (run / fall off)
4. Today is a ______________, so school is closed. (gate / holiday)
5. To be good at football, you have to ______________ often. (run / fall off)

C. Make sentences with the words in parentheses ( ) .

Example: (late) Class starts at 9:00, and it's 9:50 right now. I'm late!

1. (watch) ______________________________
2. (holiday) ______________________________
3. (run) ______________________________

Name ______________________________ Date ________________

Reading Strategy
Identify Sequence

Use with student book page 216.

To identify sequence is to see the order of events.

Academic Vocabulary for the Reading Strategy		
Word	**Explanation**	**Sample Sentence**
identify *verb*	to notice or see something	The doctor **identified** the problem and helped the patient.
sequence *noun*	the order of events	The **sequence** of events is the same every night—she comes home, does homework, eats dinner, and plays a game.

Read the story.

Mariana's Busy Day

Mariana is a sixth grader. She lives in Seattle, Washington. Last Saturday, Mariana had a very busy day. First, she woke up at 7:30. Then she ate breakfast. After breakfast, she helped her father in the yard. At 10:00, she took a shower. At 10:45, she and her father visited her grandmother. They ate lunch together, and then they went back home. Next, Mariana wrote a report and studied for a spelling test. She was tired, and she took a nap at 4:00. She woke up at 5:00. She practiced her music for the school concert. She met with her friend Cara after dinner. Finally, she read a magazine and went to sleep.

Now, identify the sequence of events. Put numbers next to the events.

_____ Mariana helped her father in the yard.

_____ Mariana went to sleep.

__1__ Mariana ate breakfast.

_____ Mariana ate dinner.

_____ Mariana wrote a report and studied for a spelling test.

_____ Mariana and her father visited her grandmother.

_____ Mariana read a magazine.

_____ Mariana took a nap.

_____ Mariana met with her friend Cara.

_____ Mariana practiced for her school concert.

Name ______________________________ Date ______________

Text Genre

Use with student book page 216.

Short Story

A short story is a narrative.

Narrative	
characters	people in the story
setting	time and place of the story
plot	what happens in a story with a beginning, middle, and end

A. Match each word with its definition.

Example: __c__ identify

1. ______ characters
2. ______ setting
3. ______ plot

a. people in the story

b. what happens in the story with a beginning, middle, and end

~~c. to notice or see something~~

d. time and place of the story

B. Read "Mariana's Busy Day" again.

Mariana's Busy Day

Mariana is a sixth grader. She lives in Seattle, Washington. Last Saturday, Mariana had a very busy day. First, she woke up at 7:30. Then she ate breakfast. After breakfast, she helped her father in the yard. At 10:00, she took a shower. At 10:45, she and her father visited her grandmother. They ate lunch together, and then they went back home. Next, Mariana wrote a report and studied for a spelling test. She was tired, and she took a nap at 4:00. She woke up at 5:00. She practiced her music for the school concert. She met with her friend Cara after dinner. Finally, she read a magazine and went to sleep.

Identify the following elements.

Example: What is the title of the story? "Mariana's Busy Day"

1. Identify the characters in the story. ______________ ______________

   ______________ ______________

2. Identify the setting of the story. ______________________________

3. Identify the plot. Circle the sentence that best describes the plot.
   a. Mariana is a sixth grader who lives in Seattle, Washington.
   b. Mariana was tired at 4:00.
   c. Mariana helped her father, visited her grandmother, and met with her friend Cara.

Name ____________________ Date ____________

Reading Comprehension

Use with student book page 220.

Answer the questions.

Example: Who are the authors of "Rain, Rain, Rain!"?

Rob Waring and Maurice Jamal

1. Why does Faye eat breakfast quickly?

2. How does Faye usually go to school?

3. Why does Faye fall off of her bike?

4. What happens when Faye gets to school?

5. What does Faye's mother try to tell her when she is leaving? Why doesn't Faye listen to her?

Name ______________________ Date ______________

Literary Element

Plot

Use with student book page 221.

The plot is what happens in a story. You can use a time line to help identify the plot. A time line lists the sequence of events.

A. Put the events in order.

_____ It's 8:45, and she is at the train station.

_____ She gets ready for school and then talks to her mother.

_____ It's 8:47, and she sees she cannot take the train to school.

_____ Faye leaves the house.

__1__ Faye sees the rain.

_____ It's 8:20 on her clock at home.

_____ It's 8:59. She is at school.

_____ It's 8:35, and she is riding her bike.

_____ Faye falls off of her bike and pushes it to the train station.

_____ She runs to school.

B. Write the events with times on the time line.

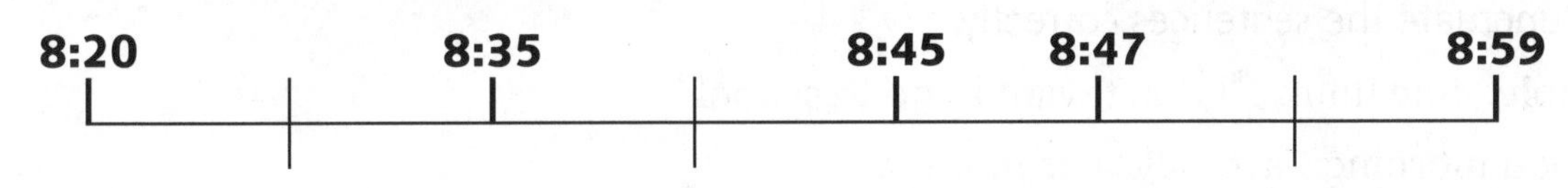

Faye is at home.

Name ______________________ Date ______________

Writing Conventions

Use with student book page 221.

Punctuation: Quotation Marks and Commas

Quotation marks (" ") show what people say. Put the first quotation mark where the speaker's words start. Put the other quotation mark where the speaker's words stop. Put a **comma** (,) between the quotation and the speaker.

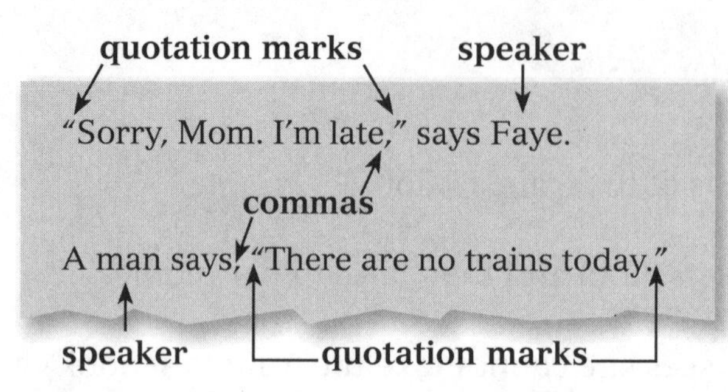

A. Identify the punctuation mistake in each sentence. Circle the type of punctuation mistake.

Example: "Hello" Tom said.	**(comma)**	**quotation mark**
1. "Where are you? Sam asked.	**comma**	**quotation mark**
2. "I'm in front of Jeff's house." Tom said.	**comma**	**quotation mark**
3. Does he live near the school?" Sam asked.	**comma**	**quotation mark**
4. "No" Tom said, "he lives near the train station."	**comma**	**quotation mark**
5. "I'll be right there, Tom." Sam said.	**comma**	**quotation mark**
6. I'll be waiting," Tom said.	**comma**	**quotation mark**

B. Punctuate the sentences correctly.

Example: She thinks, "I don't want to go to school."

1. Good morning Faye says her mother.
2. Morning Mom she says.
3. Her mother says Please sit down Faye.
4. Sorry Mom. I'm late says Faye.
5. Late? Where are you going? asks her mother.
6. School she says.
7. But Faye… says her mother.
8. Sorry Mom. I'm late. See you! says Faye.

Name ______________________ Date ______________

Vocabulary

Use with student book pages 226–227.

Clothing for All Kinds of Weather

gloves	scarf
hat	sunglasses
jacket	umbrella
raincoat	coat

A. Complete each sentence. Chose the correct word in parentheses ( ).

Example: It's cold today. Wear your ___gloves___! (sunglasses / gloves)

1. It's raining. Bring your ______________. (gloves / umbrella)
2. It's very sunny. Wear your ______________. (scarf / sunglasses)
3. I have my umbrella, but where is my ______________? (raincoat / coat)
4. It's cold outside. You need your ______________ and gloves. (umbrella / hat)
5. It's nice outside. You don't need a hat and ______________. (scarf / sunglasses)
6. It's not raining. I don't need my raincoat. I need my ______________. (scarf / jacket)

B. Unscramble the letters in parentheses. Use the vocabulary words to complete the sentences.

Example: It's cold today. Wear your ___gloves___! (sovleg)

1. You should use an ______________ when it rains. (lumlabre)
2. ______________ protect your eyes from the sun. (glunaessss)
3. Do you have a ______________? (toanraci)
4. I left my ______________ in your car yesterday. (fracs)
5. It's cold. Let me get my ______________. (catkej)

Name ______________________________ Date ______________

Vocabulary

Everyday Objects

Use with student book pages 228–229.

backpack	keys
cell phone	sunscreen
helmet	wallet

A. Write the vocabulary word under its picture.

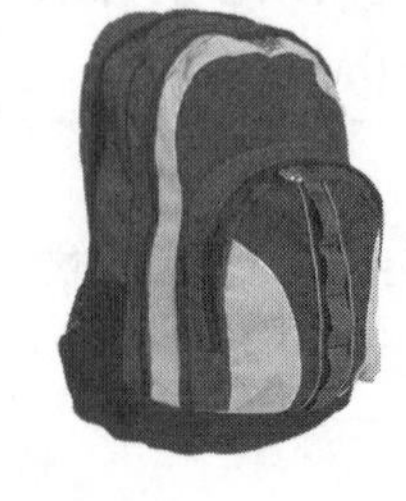

Example: Keys 1. ____________ 2. ____________

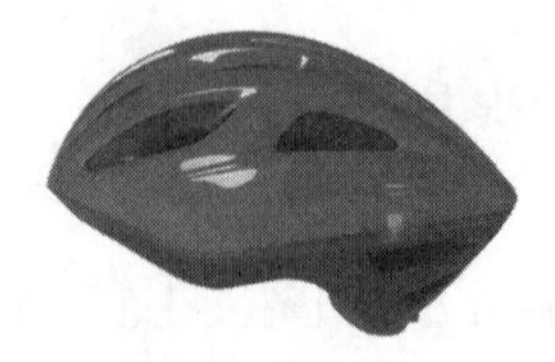

3. ____________ 4. ____________ 5. ____________

B. Remind people what they need. Match the places with the objects.

Example: d I'm going to the beach.

1. _____ I'm going shopping.
2. _____ I'm going to school.
3. _____ I'm going home and no one is there.
4. _____ I'm going to ride my bike.
5. _____ I'm calling my mother to drive me home.

a. Don't forget your backpack.
b. You need your keys.
c. Wear your helmet.
~~d. You need sunscreen.~~
e. Use your cell phone.
f. You need your wallet.

Name ______________________ Date ______________

Grammar

Imperatives

Use with student book page 230.

Use the **imperative** to give orders, instructions, directions, or reminders. The imperative is like the simple present tense without the subject.

Simple Present Tense	Imperative
You close the door.	**Close** the door. (order)
You write your name.	**Write** your name. (instruction)
You turn left.	**Turn** left. (direction)
You wear a coat.	**Wear** a coat. (reminder)

Imperative	Negative Imperative
Ride your bike.	**Don't ride** your bike.
Turn off the computer.	**Don't turn off** the computer.
Open the window.	**Don't open** the window.

A. Change the simple present sentences into imperatives.

Example: You close the door. Close the door.

1. You wear your gloves! ______________________
2. You take your books! ______________________
3. You bring your umbrella. ______________________

B. Change the imperatives to negative imperatives.

Example: Bring your cell phone. Don't bring your cell phone.

1. Bring your jacket. ______________________
2. Go to the park. ______________________

C. Write one thing to do and one thing not to do. Use imperatives and negative imperatives.

Examples: I'm going to the store. Bring your wallet. Don't leave your keys at home.

1. I'm going to school. ______________________
2. I'm going to the beach. ______________________

Name ______________________ Date ______________

Grammar

Use with student book page 231.

Object Pronouns

Pronouns are words that take the place of nouns. An **object pronoun** takes the place of an object noun.

Object Pronouns						
me	you	her	him	it	us	them

A. Underline the object noun. Write the object pronoun on the line.

Example: Give the letter to my sister. it

1. Do your homework. ______________
2. Wash the dishes. ______________
3. Take water to them. ______________
4. Give the keys to her. ______________
5. Play it for my mother. ______________

B. Read each sentence. Change the object nouns into object pronouns. Write the new sentences.

Example: Give the letter to my sister. Give it to her.

1. Give the homework to her. ______________
2. Get the money from him. ______________
3. Go visit your grandfather. ______________
4. Take it to Pedro. ______________
5. Close the window. ______________

C. Make sentences with the object nouns in parentheses ( ). Then change the object nouns into object pronouns.

Example: (letter) Mail the letter today. Mail it today.

1. (water) ______________
2. (sunscreen) ______________
3. (scarf) ______________

Name ______________________________ Date ______________

Grammar Expansion

Direct and Indirect Object Pronouns

A **direct object** receives the action of a verb.

Close the window. (*window* is the direct object)

An **indirect object** receives the direct object.

Give the water to him. (*him* is the indirect object)

Direct Object Pronouns	Indirect Object Pronouns
Close the window. Close **it.**	Give the water to Pedro. Give the water to **him.**
Wear your gloves. Wear **them.**	Take the money to Sue. Take the money to **her.**
Drink this water. Drink **it.**	She gave the test to the students. She gave the test to **them.**

A. Identify the underlined words. Circle **direct** for direct objects and **indirect** for indirect objects.

Example: Give <u>the water</u> to Pedro. **(direct)** **indirect**

1. Wear <u>these gloves</u> to the park. **direct** **indirect**
2. Play <u>basketball</u>. **direct** **indirect**
3. Write <u>a letter</u> to your best friend. **direct** **indirect**
4. Write a letter to <u>your best friend</u>. **direct** **indirect**
5. Send a gift to <u>your cousins</u>. **direct** **indirect**

B. Fill in the blanks with the correct object pronoun.

Example: Give ____it____ to ____her____. (the letter / Jennifer)

1. Take ______________ to ______________. (the water / your father)
2. Buy ______________ for ______________. (the books / your sister)
3. Send ______________ to ______________. (the scarf / your grandmother)
4. Take ______________ to ______________. (the money / your brother)

Name ______________________________ Date ____________________

Word Study

Use with student book page 232.

r-Controlled Vowel Sounds

A. Say the word for each picture. Write **ar, or, er, ir,** or **ur** to complete each word.

Example:  c ar___

1.  st___

4.   b___d

2.  col___

5.  ent___

3.   p___se

6.  c___n

B. Say the word for the picture. Circle the word that has the same **r**-controlled vowel sound.

Example:  (barn) burn born

1.  yarn horn turn

3. fern farm form

2.  cart short dirt

4.  nurse north marsh

C. Say the words. Circle the word with a different vowel sound.

Example: far  tar (for)

1. her fern corn
2. born fir dirt
3. herd yard bark
4. torn storm barn

Name ______________________ Date ______________

Writing Assignment

Write a List of Rules

Use with student book page 233.

A. Make a list of rules for your math class. Use imperatives.

Our Math Class Rules: Do

Example: Do your homework before class.

B. Make a list of rules for your math class. Use negative imperatives.

Our Math Class Rules: Don't

Example: Don't run in the classroom.

C. Answer the questions.

1. Who is the audience of the lists?

2. What is the purpose of the lists?

Name ______________________ Date ______________

Vocabulary From the Reading

Use with student book page 235.

Key Vocabulary

climate
polar
precipitation
storms
subtropical
tropical

A. Match each Key Vocabulary word with its definition.

Example: __d__ climate
1. ____ polar
2. ____ precipitation
3. ____ storms
4. ____ subtropical
5. ____ tropical

a. rain or snow
b. hot all year
c. very cold climate
~~d. the weather a place gets~~
e. usually hot, but sometimes a little cool
f. heavy wind and rain or snow

B. Match each sentence with the correct climate. Where does each person want to go?

a. tropical Hawaii
b. subtropical Hong Kong
c. polar Alaska
d. precipitation in Brazil

Example: __a__ Adam likes very hot weather.
1. ____ Juan wants to see snow.
2. ____ Carla likes to play in the rain.
3. ____ Rosa lives in a warm city.

C. Fill in each blank with the correct Key Vocabulary word.

Example: Northern Africa has a hot and dry __climate__.

1. Rain and snow are types of ______________.
2. ______________ climates are always cold.
3. Antarctica has many ______________ with snow and wind.
4. Florida is warm. It has a ______________ climate.
5. ______________ climates are hot all year.

Name ______________________ Date ______________

Reading Strategy

Identify Main Idea and Details

Use with student book page 236.

The **main idea** is the most important idea in a reading. **Details** give you more information about the main idea.

Academic Vocabulary for the Reading Strategy		
Word	**Explanation**	**Sample Sentence**
main idea *noun*	the most important idea	The **main idea** of the lesson is about different **climates** in Africa.
details *noun*	more information about the main idea	The lesson has many **details.** It talks about the desert and **tropical** and **subtropical climates** in Africa.

Read the story.

A Storm Is Coming

It was a cold December day in Connecticut. Quintin got ready for school. His mother told him, "A storm is coming." Quintin knew that his mother wanted him to wear warm clothes. He put on a sweater, warm socks, and warm pants. After he got dressed, he ate breakfast. His mother looked out of the window.

"It is very cloudy and cold," she said.

"OK. I will wear my hat, scarf, gloves, and coat."

Quintin's mother said, "Have a good day at school."

Quintin smiled. Then, he went outside.

Answer the questions about the story.

Example: What is the title of this story? "A Storm Is Coming"

1. Give details about Quintin's clothes.

____

2. Give details about the weather.

____

3. Why does Quintin put on more clothes?

____

4. What is the main idea of this story?

____

Name ______________________ Date ______________

Text Genre

Textbook

Use with student book page 236.

Textbooks give information. Science textbooks have many features to help explain information.

Textbook	
headings	titles of sections
facts	true information
graphics	photos, graphs, charts
captions	information about a picture

A. Look at this graphic from your student book. Answer the questions.

Weather Maps

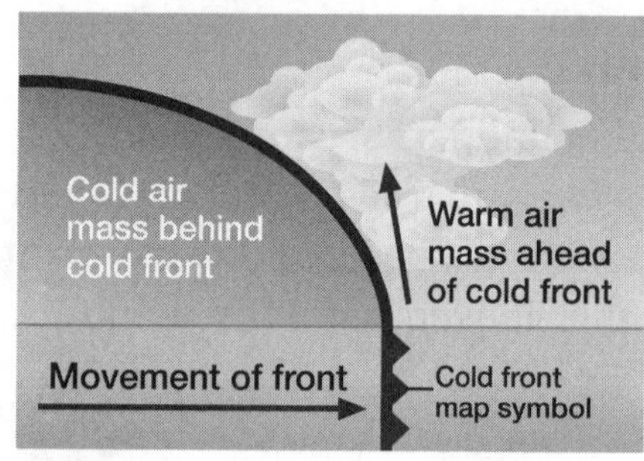

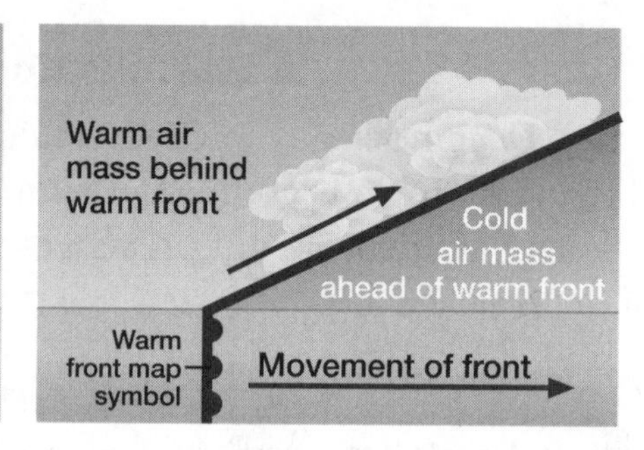

Fronts

Example: What kind of element is this? It is a graphic.

1. What is the heading? ______________________

2. What is a fact about warm fronts? ______________________

3. What does the caption say? ______________________

B. Answer these questions about textbooks.

Example: What is another name for a title of a section? heading

1. What are some examples or types of graphics? ______________________

2. What usually appears below graphics? ______________________

3. What is another name for true information? ______________________

Name ______________________ Date ______________

Reading Comprehension

Use with student book page 240.

A. Choose the correct answer.

Example: __a__ What do weather reports tell us?

a. information about weather b. information about maps

c. information about sports

1. _____ Which source does NOT have weather reports?

   a. newspaper b. dictionary c. Internet

2. _____ Which of these do weather maps NOT show?

   a. travel directions b. state borders c. temperatures across regions

3. _____ What is a warm front?

   a. a sunny day b. air that is warmer than nearby air

   c. top of a weather report

B. Answer the questions.

1. What do low pressures do to the weather?

____

____

2. How are weather and climate different?

____

____

3. What are the types of climates in the U.S.?

____

____

C. What are the summer and winter climates like where you live?

____

____

____

____

____

Name ______________________ Date ______________

Text Element

Maps

Use with student book page 241.

A map gives information about a place.

Look at the map below. Then answer the questions.

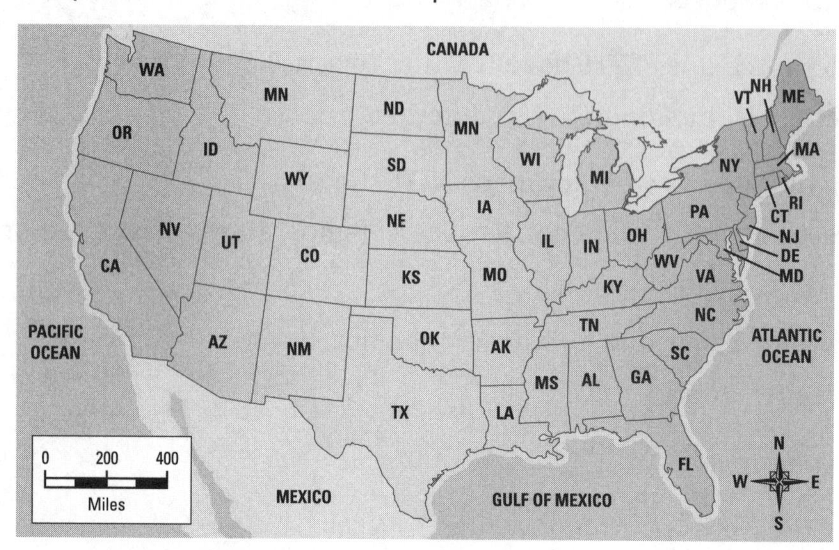

Example: How many countries are on this map? 3

1. How many U.S. states border Mexico? ______________

2. Put the abbreviation of three states that border Canada. ______________

3. To the right of FL (Florida), you see a symbol (compass) with these letters:

   W, N, E, S. What do these letters mean? ______________

   ____

4. There is a box at the bottom-left corner of the map. What is it called?

   ____

5. What is the longest state on the west side of the U.S.? ______________

6. What ocean is to the east of the U.S.? ______________

7. What ocean is to the west of the U.S.? ______________

Name ______________________ Date ______________

Vocabulary

Use with student book pages 256–257.

Rooms in Your Home

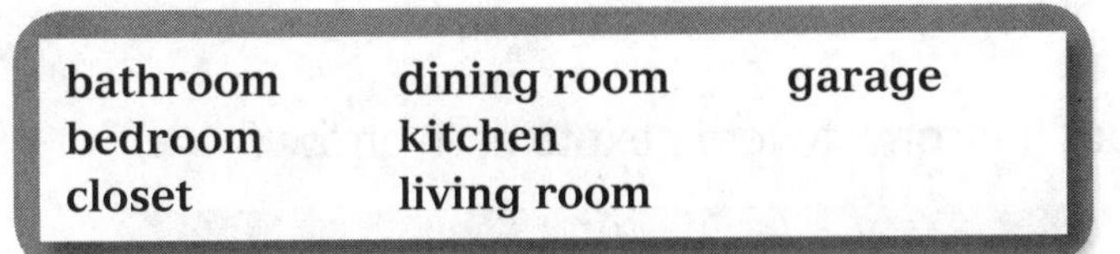

bathroom	**dining room**	**garage**
bedroom	**kitchen**	
closet	**living room**	

A. Write each room's name under its picture.

Example: dining room 1. __________ 2. __________

3. __________ 4. __________ 5. __________

B. Circle the answers.

Example: I watch TV in the ______________. (garage / (living room))

1. We eat breakfast in the ______________. (kitchen / closet)
2. His family eats dinner in the ______________. (dining room / bedroom)
3. My clothes are in the ______________. (garage / closet)
4. The car is in the ______________. (kitchen / garage)
5. I wash dishes in the ______________. (closet / kitchen)
6. She showers in the ______________. (bedroom / bathroom)
7. The baby sleeps in the ______________. (kitchen / bedroom)

Name ______________________ Date ______________

Vocabulary

Use with student book pages 258–259.

Furniture
Describing Rooms

A. Read the vocabulary words. Then put the correct word next to each arrow (⟶).

bed	**dresser**	**pillow**	**sink**	**tub**
desk	**mirror**	**shower**	**toilet**	**window**

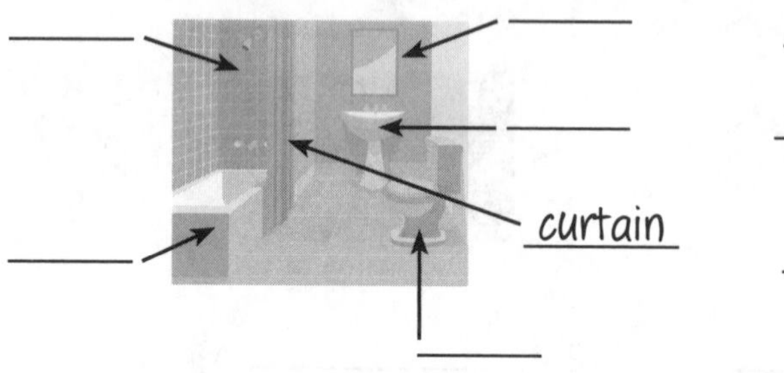

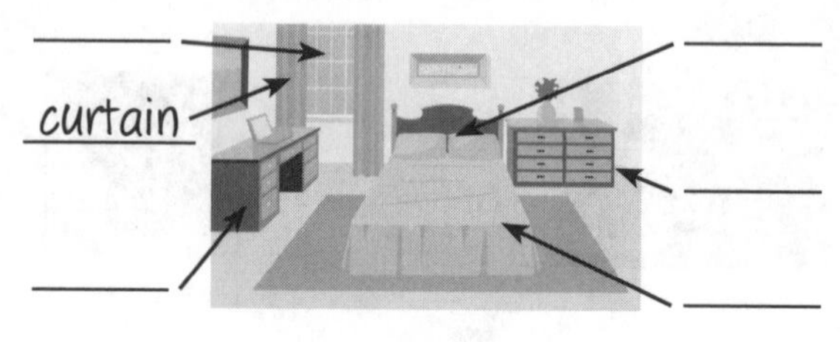

B. Make sentences about Jorge's bedroom.

In Jorge's Bedroom		Not in Jorge's Bedroom	
a bed	two pillows	refrigerator	oven
a desk	a window	sofa	bookcase

Example: *There is not a refrigerator in Jorge's bedroom.*

1. ______________________
2. ______________________
3. ______________________
4. ______________________
5. ______________________

Name ______________________ Date ______________

Grammar

Plural Nouns

Use with student book page 260.

Regular Plurals	
1.	Add **s** to the end of most words. one desk ➔ two desks a telephone ➔ four telephones
2.	Add **es** if the word ends with **s**, **x**, **z**, **sh**, or **ch**. one dish ➔ six dishes
3.	Change the **y** to **i** and add **es** if the word ends in a **consonant** + **y**. one story ➔ four stories

Nouns with Irregular Plurals

Singular Noun	Plural Noun
man, woman	men, women
person	people
child	children
foot, tooth	feet, teeth
deer, fish	deer, fish

A. Change the regular nouns in parentheses ( ) from singular to plural.

Example: There are ten ___desks___ in the room. (desk)

1. I have two ______________ in my bedroom. (bed)
2. There are two ______________ in our house. (telephone)
3. There are five ______________. (box)
4. The ______________ are eating mashed potatoes. (baby)

B. Change the irregular nouns in parentheses from singular to plural.

Example: There are two ___men___ in the room. (man)

1. Did the ______________ leave? (person)
2. The ______________ are in school. (child)
3. The ______________ are in the kitchen on the table. (knife)
4. My parents are shopping for ______________. (fish)

Name ______________________ Date ______________

Grammar

Use with student book page 261.

A, An, Some, Any

	Singular Nouns	Plural Nouns
positive statements	Use **a** or **an**. I have **a** couch. There is **an** oven.	Use **some.** I have **some** chairs. There are **some** pillows.
negative statements	Use **a** or **an**. I don't have **a** table.	Use **any.** I don't have **any** rugs. There aren't **any** ovens.
questions	Use **a** or **an**. Do you have **a** dresser? Is there **an** armchair?	Use **any.** Do you have **any** chairs? Are there **any** pillows?

A. Fill in the blanks with **a, an, some,** or **any.**

Example: There aren't ___any___ rugs in the living room.

1. There aren't ______________ pencils in the cabinet.
2. There is ______________ desk in my bedroom.
3. We don't have ______________ milk.
4. Did you give him ______________ apple?
5. I ate ______________ pizza.

B. Write sentences about a house. Use **a, an, some,** or **any** in each sentence.

Kitchen: cabinets, 1 oven, 1 refrigerator, windows, no chairs

Example: There are some cabinets.

1. ______________________________
2. ______________________________
3. ______________________________

Living Room: 2 sofas, 1 coffee table, 1 end table, no rugs

4. ______________________________
5. ______________________________
6. ______________________________

Name ______________________ Date ______________

Grammar Expansion

Questions Using Some / Any

Some and **any** are used with noncount or plural nouns. We cannot count a noncount noun. Examples of noncount nouns are **water, rice,** and **music.** In questions, use **some** when you think the answer is affirmative. Use **any** when you think the answer is negative.

Do you have some milk?	Yes, I have some milk.
Do you have any pencils?	No, I don't have any pencils.

A. Complete the sentences. Use **some** or **any.**

1. Do you have any games? No, I don't have ____________ games.
2. Would you like ____________ rice? Yes, I would like some rice.
3. Do you have any ideas? Yes, I have ____________ ideas.
4. Do you have ____________ money? No, I don't have any money.
5. Can I play ____________ music? Yes, please play some music.
6. Would you like some milk? No, I would not like ____________ milk.
7. Do you have ____________ pencils? Yes, I have some pencils.

B. Write questions. Use the words in parentheses.

Example: (we / some / fruit) Do we have some fruit?

1. (they / some / water) ____________
2. (you / some / chairs) ____________
3. (I / any / orange juice) ____________
4. (she / any / pencils) ____________
5. (he / some / socks) ____________
6. (they / any / vegetables) ____________
7. (we / any / milk) ____________

Name ______________________________ Date ________________

Word Study

Use with student book pages 262–263.

Silent e
Vowel digraph: -oo- and u

A. Read each pair of words aloud. Circle the word with the long vowel sound.

Example: cap / (cape)

1. ate / at
2. hide / hid
3. rod / rode
4. cube / cub
5. not / note
6. dim / dime
7. use / us
8. cape / cap
9. hop / hope
10. can / cane

B. Read each sentence. Circle each word that has the -oo- sound. You can circle more than one word in each sentence.

Example: The box is (full) of (wool).

1. You should read this book.
2. The big bull hurt a hoof.
3. The good dog says, "Woof."
4. The red hood is made of wool.
5. He could chop the wood.
6. Push the cookie to me.
7. I stood on one foot.
8. The cook made a full pot.
9. He shook the green bush.
10. Who took my rook?

C. Unscramble the words.

Example:  doho hood

1. 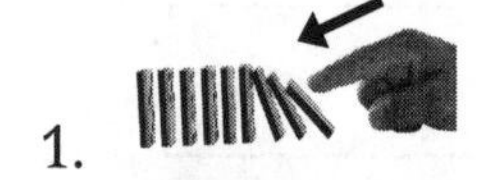

suhp ______________

2. 

epac ______________

3. 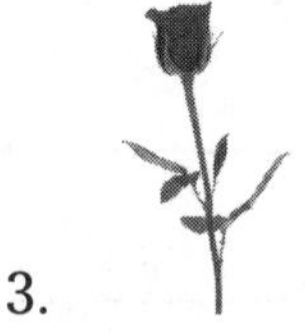

oesr ______________

4. 

lubl ______________

Name ______________________________ Date ______________

Word Study

Use with student book page 264.

Suffixes: er, or, ist

er = a person or thing that does something
or = a person who does something
ist = a person who does something

A. Write the definition for each word.

Example: A teacher is a person who teaches.

1. A worker is ______________.
2. A pianist is ______________.
3. A visitor is ______________.
4. A computer is ______________.

B. Write the correct spelling of each word.

Example: denter dentor dentist dentist

1. teacher teachor teachist ______________
2. docter doctor doctist ______________
3. player playor playist ______________
4. actor acter actist ______________

C. Write a word from the box to finish each sentence.

Example: The cyclist rode her bicycle for twenty miles.

banker	cyclist	inventor	sailor
biologist	farmer	singer	

1. The ______________ will sing at the concert tonight.
2. The smart ______________ invented a new kind of telephone.
3. My mom is a ______________ at the bank.
4. The ______________ knows a lot about biology.
5. We visited the ______________ on his farm.
6. I want to be a ______________ and have a sailboat.

Name ______________________ Date ______________

Writing Assignment

Descriptive Paragraph

Use with student book page 265.

A. Choose a room in your house to describe. Make a list of the things in the room.

Example:	My Living Room		
2 bookcases	1 coffee table	4 windows	10 pillows

My ______			

B. Make sentences from the information above.

Example: There are two bookcases in my living room. There are also a desk, a chair, and three lamps.

____

____

____

____

____

____

____

____

____

Name ______________________ Date ______________

Vocabulary From the Reading

Use with student book page 267.

Key Vocabulary

angry	contest	weave
behave	spider	

A. Match each Key Vocabulary word with its meaning.

Example: e weave — a. to act in a certain way

1. ____ behave — b. a small animal with eight legs
2. ____ contest — c. mad
3. ____ spider — d. comparing peoples' skills
4. ____ angry — ~~e. to make cloth with yarn or string~~

B. Fill in the blanks with the correct Key Vocabulary word.

Example: I am not happy. I am angry.

1. The child was afraid of the ______________ on the bed.
2. Our dogs ______________ very well.
3. The school's math team won first place in the ______________.
4. They ______________ cloth from silk thread.
5. My aunt was not ______________ when I broke the glass.

C. Make your own sentences. Use the Key Vocabulary words in parentheses.

Example: (weave) The children learned to weave cloth from cotton.

1. (angry) ______________________________
2. (behave) ______________________________
3. (spider) ______________________________

Name ______________________ Date ______________

Reading Strategy

Use with student book page 268.

Recognize Cause and Effect

A **cause** is the reason something happens. The **effect** is what happens because of the cause.

Word	Explanation	Sample Sentence
cause	a reason something happens	The **cause** of the accident was a loose nail.
effect	the result of something else	The **effect** of his hard work was he passed his test easily!

A. Underline the cause and circle the effect.

Example: I was in a hurry, so I forgot my wallet.

1. I was up late last night because I had a lot of homework.
2. His keys are on the table, so he can't get into the house.
3. She ate because she was hungry.
4. Their kitchen is small, so there aren't any table and chairs.

B. Read the story. Underline the causes.

Problems

One day, John woke up late. He had many problems that day. First, he had no time for a hot breakfast, so he ate cold cereal. Next, he ran out of the house. He forgot to bring his lunch with him. At lunchtime, his friends shared their food with him. When he got home, he didn't have his key to the house. He waited by the door. Later, his mother was angry. She said, "Next time, wake up earlier!"

C. Now write the causes and the effects in the boxes.

Cause	Effect
Example: John woke up late.	He had many problems that day.
1.	
2.	
3.	
4.	

Name ______________________ Date ______________

Text Genre

Myth

Use with student book page 268.

A **myth** is a story. It is not true. Myths usually explain why something is the way it is in nature. Characters in myths may have special powers.

Myth	
characters with special powers	people in myths can often do things that real people can't do
explanation	a reason why something in nature is the way it is

Read the myth.

Clouds

Zeus is a Greek god. He is the king of the gods and goddesses. Apollo is the god of the sky. He carries the sun so we can have sunlight. One day, Apollo asked Zeus to celebrate a holiday. Zeus asked everyone where it should be. He asked one family named Sky. The Sky family wanted to celebrate the holiday in the air. Zeus agreed. He turned the Sky family into clouds. Then the gods and goddesses celebrated the holiday on top of the clouds. When you see clouds, that means Zeus and the other gods and goddesses are having a holiday celebration.

Now answer the questions.

Example: What is the title of this myth? Clouds

1. Is this a true story? ______________________
2. Who is Zeus? ______________________
3. Who is Apollo and what is his special power? ______________________
4. What is the explanation of this myth? ______________________

Name ______________________ Date ______________

Reading Comprehension

Use with student book page 272.

A. Choose the correct answer. Write the letter in the blank.

Example: __a__ What does a weaver make?

a. cloth b. food c. myths

1. _____ What is the setting of the story?
   a. 3,000 years ago in Rome
   b. 200 years ago in America
   c. 2,000 years ago in Greece

2. _____ Who is Athena?
   a. a goddess b. a man c. a spider

3. _____ Who is Arachne?
   a. a goddess b. a teacher c. a weaver

B. Answer the questions.

1. Why did Athena turn Arachne into a spider?

____

____

____

____

____

2. What does this myth explain?

____

____

____

____

____

Name ______________________ Date ______________

Literary Elements

Problem and Solution

Use with student book page 273.

A **problem** is something that causes difficulty. A **solution** stops or solves the problem.

A. Identify the problem and the solution. Write them in the correct place.

Example: Two children need a nap, but there is only one pillow. They share the pillow.

Problem: Two children need a nap, but there is only one pillow.

Solution: They share the pillow.

1. They go to the store to buy more. The family has no sunscreen.

Problem: ______________________

Solution: ______________________

2. They fix the window. The father and son broke the living room window.

Problem: ______________________

Solution: ______________________

3. They are tired. They take a nap.

Problem: ______________________

Solution: ______________________

4. They study. They have a test.

Problem: ______________________

Solution: ______________________

5. The baby is crying. They feed the baby.

Problem: ______________________

Solution: ______________________

Name ______________________ Date ______________

Writing Conventions

Use with student book page 273.

Spelling Homophones: two, to, too

Homophones	Sentence
two = 2 (number)	I have **two** pillows.
to = part of a verb = preposition	You need **to** eat. She went **to** the store.
too = also	He has a book. I have a book, **too**.

A. Fill in the blanks with the correct word. Use **two, to,** or **too.**

Example: I have ___two___ lamps on my desk.

1. Do you like to listen __________ music?
2. There were __________ apples on the kitchen table.
3. He wants __________ go, __________!
4. Did you find __________ gloves in the car or only one?
5. Are you going __________ the shopping mall?
6. I have __________ study for my history test.
7. I like the red one __________, so buy them both.
8. There are __________ sofas in the living room.
9. He needs __________ clean his room.
10. Why do you like __________ use green pens so often?

B. Now make your own sentences with the homophones in parentheses.

Example: (two) I have two lamps on my desk.

1. (two) ______________________________
2. (to) ______________________________
3. (too) ______________________________
4. (two) ______________________________
5. (to) ______________________________
6. (too) ______________________________

Name ______________________ Date ______________

Vocabulary

Food and Drinks

Use with student book pages 278–279.

drinks	fruits	grains	meat	proteins	vegetables

A. Write the correct vocabulary word for each picture.

Example:

fruits and vegetables

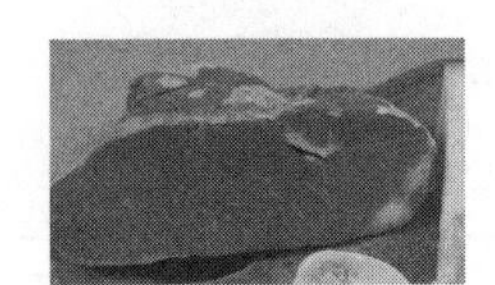

1. ____________

2. ____________

3. ____________

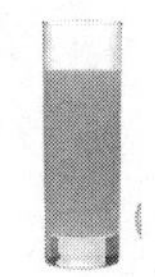

4. ____________

B. Use the words below to fill in the chart.

banana	broccoli	cheese	fish	lettuce	orange
beef	carrot	chicken	~~grapes~~	meat	rice
bread	cereal	egg	~~juice~~	milk	water

Drinks	Fruits	Grains	Meat	Proteins	Vegetables
juice	grapes				

Name ______________________ Date ______________

Vocabulary

Use with student book pages 280–281.

Other Foods and Dishes
Saying What You Have and Need

bowl	**glass**	**mustard**	**plate**	**spoon**
butter	**ketchup**	**oil**	**salsa**	
fork	**knife**	**pepper**	**salt**	

A. Fill in the blanks. Use the letters in parentheses.

Father: Please put the (1) ____________ (kfro), (2) ____________ (opons), and (3) ____________ (efkin) by the (4) ____________ (eatlp).

Mother: Don't forget a (5) ____________ (wlbo) and a (6) ____________ (sslag), too.

Jorge: Please pass me the (7) ____________ (turbet) and (8) ____________ (ilo). Thank you.

Father: Please pass me the (9) ____________ (aalss), and also the (10) ____________ (tlsa) and (11) ____________ (eepppr). Thank you.

B. Answer the questions.

Example: What do you use to eat eggs? a fork and plate

1. What do you use to eat soup? ____________
2. What do you use to eat fish? ____________
3. What do you use to drink lemonade? ____________
4. What do you use to eat broccoli? ____________
5. What do you use to eat salad? ____________
6. What do you put on potatoes? ____________
7. What do you put on ground beef? ____________
8. What do you put on bread? ____________

Name ______________________ Date ______________

Grammar

Use with student book pages 282–283.

Count and Noncount Nouns

Count nouns are things you can count. They have a singular form and a plural form. Noncount nouns are things you cannot count.

Count Nouns	Noncount Nouns
an egg / 2 eggs	rice
one apple / 3 apples	milk
a pear / 6 pears	some butter

A. Write **C** for count and **N** for noncount nouns.

Example: __C__ apple

1. _____ butter
2. _____ cheese
3. _____ lamp
4. _____ sink
5. _____ soup
6. _____ spoon
7. _____ sugar
8. _____ table
9. _____ salad
10. _____ sandwich

B. Complete the shopping list of nouns. Write **a, an,** or **some** to show if they are count or noncount nouns.

My Shopping List		
__a__ banana	____ beef	____ tomato
____ carrot	____ mushroom	____ bread
____ sugar	____ cereal	____ apple

C. Rewrite the incorrect sentences to make them correct. If a sentence is correct, write **correct.**

Example: You gave me a forks. You gave me a fork.

1. Can I have a cheese? ______________________
2. There are some fork and knives on the table. ______________________
3. Can I have some salt and pepper? ______________________
4. We need some rices, an tomatoes, and three potato. ______________________
5. May I have a bowl of cereal? ______________________

Name ______________________ Date ______________

D. Fill in the blanks with **is** or **are** and the words in parentheses to describe the nouns.

Example: There are five apples in the bowl. (five)

1. There ______________ students playing basketball over there. (some)
2. There ______________ ketchup on the table. (some)
3. There ______________ sisters with curly hair in that car. (two)
4. There ______________ rulers and calculators in the cabinet. (twenty-five)
5. There ______________ apple in my backpack. (an)
6. There ______________ salsa for those chips. (some)
7. There ______________ orange on the table. (an)
8. There ______________ students in my class. (fifteen)

E. Put the words in the correct order.

Example: (eat / after / I / some / grapes / always / school.)
I always eat some grapes after school.

1. (spoons / are / sink. / There / in / the / some) ______________
2. (sofa. / is / a / There / on / the / jacket) ______________
3. (have / don't / We / milk. / any) ______________
4. (need / cheese / I / sandwich. / some / my / for) ______________
5. (any / for / cereal? / Is / milk / there / my) ______________
6. (in / rulers / some / cabinet. / There / are / the) ______________
7. (plates? / you / any / have / Do) ______________
8. (some / I / May / apples? / have) ______________

Name ______________________ Date ______________________

Grammar Expansion

Quantifiers

A quantifier is a word or phrase that describes size or number. It is not a number. **Much** and **many** mean a large amount. **A few** and **a little** mean a small amount.

Count Nouns	Noncount Nouns
I have **many** pencils.	We don't have **much** rice.
I have **a few** pencils.	We have **a little** rice.

A. Circle the correct quantifier.

Example: I don't have ________ time. — (much) many

1. They have ________ telephones in their house. — **much** **many**
2. There are ________ windows in the living room. — **much** **many**
3. We didn't eat ________ meat. — **much** **many**
4. The children played ________ basketball today. — **a few** **a little**
5. There are ________ kinds of juice in his refrigerator. — **a few** **a little**
6. I like ________ butter on my bread. — **a few** **a little**

B. Complete the sentences with the correct quantifier.

Example: I don't have ___much___ time.

1. You have ________ keys. I count 15 keys on your key ring.
2. We only have ________ broccoli. I think we need more.
3. My father doesn't drink ________ juice. He says it's too sweet.
4. You only need ________ peaches to make a pie.
5. I don't like ________ meat on my sandwiches.
6. I like ________ milk on my cereal.

Name ______________________ Date ______________

Word Study
Long a

Use with student book page 284.

A. Write the word that has the long **a** sound.

Example: man mane mane

1. tap tape ________
2. rain ran ________
3. lack lake ________
4. ray ran ________
5. when weigh ________
6. tale tall ________
7. mad made ________
8. paid pad ________
9. mall male ________
10. ate at ________

B. Write **a, e, ay,** or **ai** to finish each word.

Example:  lemon a d e

1.  l __ k __

2.  r __ k __

3.  t __ l

4.  tr __

5.  br __ d

6.  h __

Name ______________________ Date ______________

Writing Assignment

Use with student book page 285.

Descriptive Essay

A. Make a list of the foods you like.

Example:

Eun-Byul's Favorite Foods					
Fruit	Vegetables	Grains	Proteins	Meat	Drinks
grapes	broccoli	pasta	cheese	chicken	milk

My Favorite Foods					
Fruit	Vegetables	Grains	Proteins	Meat	Drinks

B. Answer the questions about your family.

Example: What vegetable does your family often eat? broccoli

1. What fruit does your family often eat? ______
2. What vegetable does your family often eat? ______
3. What grain does your family often eat? ______
4. What protein does your family often eat? ______
5. What meat does your family often eat? ______
6. What drink does your family often drink? ______

C. Write three sentences about the things that your family often eats.

1. ______
2. ______
3. ______

Name ______________________________ Date ____________________

Vocabulary From the Reading

Use with student book page 287.

Key Vocabulary

liberty	national	symbol
monument	represent	

A. Match the Key Vocabulary word with its definition.

Example: __b__ liberty — a. to show or describe something

1. _____ monument — b. a statue to remember a person or event
2. _____ national — c. something that shows or describes something else
3. _____ represent — ~~d. ability to do many things~~
4. _____ symbol — e. of a nation or country

B. Read the sentences. Put the answers in the crossword puzzle boxes.

ACROSS

1. I have the __liberty__ to speak my opinion.
2. Their __________ song is "O Canada."
3. Governments __________ their people.

DOWN

4. $ is a __________ for dollars.
5. The Washington __________ is in Washington, D.C.

								4
		1 L	I	B	E	R	T	Y
	5							
	2							
3								

Name ______________________ Date ______________

Reading Strategy

Take Notes

Use with student book page 288.

Taking **notes** helps you identify what you read. A **graphic organizer** can help you organize your notes.

Academic Vocabulary for the Reading Strategy

Word	Explanation	Sample Sentence
notes	short written reminders of what you have read or heard	Brad takes **notes** when he reads his homework.
graphic organizer	a way to picture information	Lin drew a **graphic organizer** of the main ideas.

Read the paragraph.

How to Make a Perfect Sandwich

There are many things you need to make the perfect sandwich. First, you must start with good bread. Make sure the pieces of bread aren't too thick. Next, put on a condiment such as mustard or mayonnaise. Don't put on too much or you will make a mess. Tomato and lettuce are important because they are healthy. You also need protein. Don't forget to put on your favorite meat or cheese!

Now take notes on the important ideas. Keep your notes short. Do not write sentences.

Example: bread

a. use good bread

b. slices not too thick

1. ______________________

   a. ______________________

   b. ______________________

2. ______________________

   a. ______________________

   b. ______________________

3. ______________________

   a. ______________________

   b. ______________________

Name ________________________ Date ____________

Text Genre

Expository Text

Use with student book page 288.

Expository text explains or describes an event or situation.

Expository Text	
subject	what the text is about
facts	true information
explanations	tell how someone does something
captions	words under a picture or illustration to explain what it is

Read the information.

The **Liberty** Bell was first rung in 1776.

The Liberty Bell

The 2,000-pound Pennsylvania State House Bell was first called the Liberty Bell by a group trying to stop slavery*. It was their symbol for freedom. On July 8, 1776, the Liberty Bell rang from the tower of Independence Hall. It called the people to hear the first reading of the Declaration of Independence. The Liberty Bell last rang for George Washington's birthday in 1846.

***slavery:** when people are made to work for no money by another group of people

Now answer the questions.

Example: How much does the liberty bell weigh? 2,000 pounds

1. What is the subject of the text? ____________

2. List three facts about the Liberty Bell. ____________

____

____

3. Explain what the bell did. ____________

____

4. What does the caption say? ____________

____

Name ______________________ Date ______________

Reading Comprehension

Use with student book page 292.

A. Choose the correct answer. Write the letter in the blank.

Example: __a__ When did the bald eagle become the national bird?

a. 1782 b. 1762 c. 1795

1. _____ Which is NOT an example of a national symbol?

   a. American flag b. Statue of Liberty c. newspaper

2. _____ Where is the Capitol building?

   a. Philadelphia b. Washington, D.C. c. New York

3. _____ Where is the Great Seal?

   a. one-dollar bill b. president's office c. Philadelphia

B. What does the Statue of Liberty symbolize to immigrants?

____

____

____

____

____

C. Identify the symbols in the American flag. Explain their meanings.

____

____

____

____

____

Name ______________________ Date ______________

Text Elements

Use with student book page 293.

Photos and Illustrations

A **photo** is a photograph of a real object. An **illustration** is an artist's drawing. Photos and illustrations can help you understand the main idea of the text. A **caption** is the words next to or below the photo or illustration. It explains what the picture is or where it is from.

1.

Uncle Sam often walks in **parades.**

2.

Living room

3.

The Lopez Family Tree.

4.

The boys had a running **contest.** Joe won.

Look at the graphics above. Answer the questions.

Example: How many illustrations are there? two

1. Which two graphics are photos? ______________________
2. Which two graphics are illustrations? ______________________
3. What is the caption of picture in Number 1? ______________________

   ____
4. What is the caption of picture in Number 3? ______________________

   ____

Name ______________________ Date ______________

Vocabulary
Occupations

Use with student book pages 308–309.

cashier	**doctor**	**mail carrier**
chef	**firefighter**	**police officer**
construction worker	**hairstylist**	

A. Match each occupation with its description.

Example: h cashier

1. ____ chef
2. ____ construction worker
3. ____ doctor
4. ____ firefighter
5. ____ hairstylist
6. ____ mail carrier
7. ____ police officer

a. takes care of sick people
b. builds houses and buildings
c. prepares and cooks food
d. delivers mail
e. cuts and styles people's hair
f. protects people
g. fights fires
~~h. takes money and gives change~~

B. Match the occupation with the workplace.

Example: I am a hairstylist. I work at a salon.

1. I am a ______________. I work in a restaurant.
2. Jeff is a ______________. He works for the post office.
3. Jackie is a ______________. She works at a store.
4. Manuela is a ______________. She works at a hospital.
5. Woo-Yul is a ______________. He puts out fires in the city.
6. They are ______________. They are building a new high school.

Name ______________________ Date ______________

Vocabulary

Tools and Equipment

Use with student book pages 310–311.

cash register	flashlight	tools
clipboard	scissors	utensils
fire extinguisher	stethoscope	

A. Identify the tools and equipment.

Example: clipboard 1. __________ 2. __________ 3. __________

4. __________ 5. __________ 6. __________ 7. __________

B. Fill in the blanks.

Example: A cashier uses a cash register.

1. A doctor uses a __________.
2. A firefighter uses a __________.
3. A construction worker uses __________.
4. A chef uses __________.
5. A hairstylist uses __________.

C. Complete the sentences. Unscramble the letters in parentheses.

punctual	hardworking	~~chef~~	job	restaurant

Bob is a **(example)** chef (fhec). His
(1) __________ (rtaaseuntr) is near the park. He is very
(2) __________ (wgrohindrak). He is never late for his
(3) __________ (bjo). He is always
(4) __________ (tupualnc).

Name ______________________ Date ______________

Grammar
Adjectives

Use with student book page 312.

Adjectives describe nouns. They come before the nouns they describe.

A. Match the adjectives and nouns.

Example: c sad

1. _____ fun
2. _____ cold
3. _____ large
4. _____ hot
5. _____ nice

a. teacher (She is patient with her students.)
b. water (It is good to drink with ice on a hot day.)
c. ~~boy (He lost his toy truck.)~~
d. classroom (There are 60 desks in the room.)
e. music class (We play the drums, piano, and guitar.)
f. day (It is summer; let's go swimming.)

B. Make sentences with the nouns and adjectives in parentheses. Use the verbs **be, feel, look,** and **seem.**

Example: (test / hard) The test last week was hard.

1. (day / hot) ______________________
2. (girl / sad) ______________________
3. (dog / friendly) ______________________
4. (house / nice) ______________________
5. (water / cold) ______________________
6. (jacket / warm) ______________________
7. (mail carrier / reliable) ______________________
8. (chef / creative) ______________________
9. (doctor / caring) ______________________
10. (cashier / hardworking) ______________________

Name ______________________ Date ______________

Grammar

Adverbs

Use with student book pages 312–313.

Adverbs tell how something is done.

A. Underline the adverbs.

Example: The little girl walked happily to the store.

1. The middle school students sang beautifully in the school concert.
2. The mother waited patiently for her sons to clean their messy rooms.
3. The little boy tied his shoes successfully for the first time yesterday.
4. The family ate slowly because the food was terrible.
5. The patient doctor explained the problem simply to the old woman.
6. The dog walked lazily on that hot day.

B. Put the words in the correct order.

Example: (happily / The / girl / walked / to / little / the / store.)

The little girl walked happily to the store.

1. (children / late / quickly / ran / The / to / school.)

____

2. (song / played / She / violin. / sadly / on / the / the)

____

3. (angrily. / the / door / closed / He)

____

4. (The / father / baby. / the / down / put / sleeping / carefully)

____

5. (happily / The / store. / walked / to / girl / the / little)

____

Name ______________________ Date ______________

Grammar Expansion

More Adverbs

Adverbs describe verbs and adjectives.

Rule	Adverb	Example
1. Some adverbs have the same form as the adjective.	*hard, fast*	She threw the ball **fast.**
2. Some adverbs describe adjectives or other adverbs.	*very, really, kind of*	They did **very** well on the test.
3. Some adverbs explain time or location.	*here, there* *yesterday, today, now*	Put it **here** on the table. **Yesterday,** I went to the dentist.
4. To change **-ic** adjectives to adverbs, add *-ally.*	*basically, mathematically*	I think **mathematically.**

A. Look at the chart above. Find the explanation for how the adverb is used or formed in each sentence. Then put the number of the explanation on the line.

Example: __2__ They did **very** well on the test.

1. _____ The dog ran **fast.**
2. _____ She went **yesterday.**
3. _____ He came **here.**
4. _____ I was **really** happy.
5. _____ Let's go **tomorrow.**
6. _____ He **basically** knows.
7. _____ She is **kind of** angry.
8. _____ I studied **hard.**

B. Underline the adverbs.

Example: The test was <u>very</u> difficult.

1. Did he go today or yesterday?
2. The class is mathematically advanced.
3. That car is really bright blue.
4. It is here in the cabinet.

Name ______________________________ Date ____________________

Word Study

Use with student book pages 314–315.

Vowel: Long o
Vowel: Long i

A. Circle the word with the long vowel sound. Write the long vowel sound.

Example: (home) him __o__

1. stone cap ____
2. boat tap ____
3. slide hood ____
4. snow corn ____
5. fly bird ____
6. push kite ____
7. ice purse ____
8. road cat ____
9. nose fern ____
10. night star ____

B. Say the word for each picture. Circle the item with the same vowel sound.

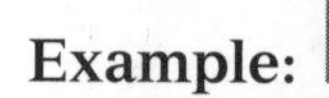
Example:  (Web site) snow

1. 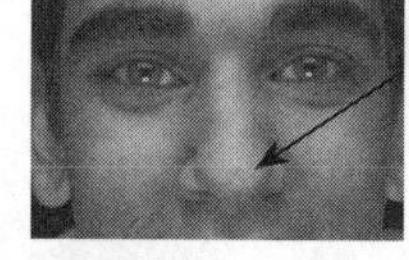 stone full

2.  enter dry

3.  star fight

4.  fine most

5.  post nine

6.  rice bird

7.  mile grow

8.  girl hose

9.  tight corn

10.  mow tide

Name ______________________ Date ______________

Word Study

Use with student book page 316.

Prefixes: pre, post, re

Prefixes	Examples
pre = before	prefix, **pre**heat, **pre**record
post = after	**post**test
re = again	**re**group, **re**tell

Read the words. Make a new word with the prefix **pre, post,** or **re.** Write the word in the crossword puzzle.

Across

1. build again
2. meeting after the game
3. soak in water before washing
5. cut before using
6. meeting before the game
7. write a date that is after now

Down

1. draw one more time
2. test after the lesson
4. use over again

1 r e b u i l d

Name ______________________ Date ______________

Writing Assignment

Descriptive Narrative

Use with student book page 317.

A. Answer the questions to help brainstorm your topic.

Example: Who will you write about? Uncle Frank

1. Who will you write about? ______________________
2. Where does the person live? ______________________
3. How do you know the person? ______________________
4. What job does the person have? ______________________
5. What do you like the most about the person? ______________________

B. Now give details. List nouns and adjectives to describe the person you will write about.

Example:

Name: Uncle Frank		
uncle	funny	teacher

Name: ______		

C. Now give more details. Write three sentences about the person.

1. ______________________
2. ______________________
3. ______________________

Name ______________________ Date ______________

Vocabulary From the Reading

Use with student book page 319.

Key Vocabulary
community
court
elect
fare
fingerprints

A. Match each Key Vocabulary word with its definition.

Example: __e__ community

1. _____ court
2. _____ elect
3. _____ fare
4. _____ fingerprints

a. to choose someone for something by voting for him or her

b. money you pay to ride a bus, train, or taxi

c. a place where decisions are made about people who may have broken the law

d. prints from small lines on your fingers

~~e. a group of people, such as those that live in a town, or with similar interests~~

B. Fill in the blanks with the correct Key Vocabulary word.

Example: The criminal went to ____court____ to learn his punishment for breaking the law.

1. The Chinese ______________ has a big celebration for Chinese New Year.
2. He paid the train ______________.
3. The students voted to ______________ Sandra for class president.
4. The police took his ______________ at the police station.

C. Now make sentences with the words in parentheses.

Example: (court) The bank robber had to go to court.

1. (fare) ______________
2. (community) ______________
3. (elect) ______________
4. (fingerprints) ______________

Name ______________________ Date ______________

Reading Strategy

Use with student book page 320.

Ask Information Questions While You Read

Questions that begin with **when, why, where, what,** and **who** are examples of information questions. Ask questions as you read and find the answers.

Academic Vocabulary for the Reading Strategy		
Phrase	**Explanation**	**Sample Sentence**
when question	asks about time	"When did it happen?"
why question	asks about a reason	"Why did he come?"
where question	asks about a place	"Where did they go?"

A. Read only the title of the paragraph below. Then write questions that you think the paragraph will answer. Use the question words given to help you think of questions.

Example: Who was rescued?

1. What ______________________
2. When ______________________
3. Where ______________________
4. Why ______________________
5. How ______________________

The Rescue

Kathy was alone at her house. Her house was on fire! A neighbor called the fire station. The firefighters came quickly. They helped Kathy get out of her house with a ladder. The firefighters rescued Kathy!

B. Now write more questions. What else do you want to know about the story?

Example: What did the firefighters say about Kathy?

1. ______________________
2. ______________________
3. ______________________
4. ______________________

Name ______________________ Date ______________

Text Genre

Play

Use with student book page 320.

A play is a story presented to an audience. Plays have characters, a setting, and a plot.

Play	
audience	people who watch a play
scene	part of a play that happens at one time
lines	what the actors say
stage directions	notes in the play that tell the actors how to speak and move
narrator	a person who gives the scene and background information
character	a person in play

Read the lines from this play for middle school students.

Scene 2: A Restaurant

NARRATOR: The family is eating dinner at a neighborhood restaurant. (*The WAITER enters from the kitchen.*)

FATHER: We would like some more water, please.

WAITER: Yes, sir. Right away.

Answer the questions about the play.

Example: What is the name of the scene? A Restaurant

1. What is the waiter's line? ______________________
2. What is the scene's stage direction? ______________________
3. What does the narrator say? ______________________
4. Who is the audience? ______________________

Name ______________________________ Date ________________

Reading Comprehension

Use with student book page 326.

A. Choose the correct answer. Write the letter in the blank.

Example: __a__ What is the title of the play?

a. Enter Rosa Parks b. Rosa Parks c. Rosa Parks' Story

1. _____ What is the setting of the play?

   a. 1920s. San Diego, California b. 1860s. Atlanta, Georgia
   c. 1950s. Montgomery, Alabama

2. _____ What did the police do to Rosa Parks?

   a. nothing b. arrested her c. let her go

3. _____ How does E.D. Nixon feel about segregation laws?

   a. They are wrong. b. They are right. c. He doesn't know.

4. _____ How did the black community want to stop bus segregation?

   a. pay more money b. go home c. boycott the buses

B. Answer the questions.

1. The bus driver said, "Hey, y'all in the back! I need those seats." Why did he say it? What did he mean?

   ____

   ____

   ____

2. Why do you think black taxi drivers charged black riders the same fare as the buses?

   ____

   ____

   ____

Name ______________________ Date ______________

Literary Element

Use with student book page 327.

Figurative Language: Similes

Authors sometimes use **figurative language** in their writing. Figurative language can help the reader see or feel what's happening in the reading. A **simile** is one kind of figurative language. Similes use the words **like** or **as** to compare things.

A. Identify the similes. Circle **simile** if the sentence contains a simile, and **not a simile** if it does not.

Example: Her feet are tired. **simile** **not a simile** (circled)

1. She is as brave as a lion. **simile** **not a simile**
2. He is quiet like a cat. **simile** **not a simile**
3. Their smiles are bright and happy. **simile** **not a simile**
4. The children ran in every direction like ants. **simile** **not a simile**
5. His voice is an airplane engine. **simile** **not a simile**
6. Her skin is as soft as a baby's. **simile** **not a simile**

B. Explain the similes. Use adjectives.

Example: Her feet are like lead. Her feet and lead are both heavy.

1. She is as brave as a lion. ______________________
2. The children ran like ants. ______________________
3. His voice is like an airplane engine. ______________________
4. Her skin is as soft as a baby's. ______________________

C. Make a simile with the words in parentheses.

Example: (feet / lead) Her feet are like lead.

1. (busy / bee) ______________________
2. (slow / snail) ______________________
3. (quick / rabbit) ______________________

Name ______________________ Date ______________

Writing Conventions

Use with student book page 327.

Capitalization: Creative Works, Organizations, Historical Periods and Special Events

Use capital letters for each word in creative works: titles of books, names of plays, famous works of art, names of songs, and so on. Use capital letters for names of groups and organizations, historical periods and special events, also. Do not capitalize the words **the** or **a/an,** unless they are the first word in the title. Do not capitalize prepositions (**for, to, on**) or conjunctions (**and, but, or**) unless they are the first word in the title.

A. Read the list of creative works and organizations. Identify the correct and incorrect capitalization. Circle **correct** or **incorrect.**

Example: the Color Purple	**correct**	**(incorrect)**
1. The Environmental Protection Agency	**correct**	**incorrect**
2. The Color Of Water	**correct**	**incorrect**
3. The American Revolution	**correct**	**incorrect**
4. The mona lisa	**correct**	**incorrect**
5. the Boston Police department	**correct**	**incorrect**
6. The New York Times	**correct**	**incorrect**
7. New York City marathon	**correct**	**incorrect**

B. Read the list of creative works. Write each one using correct capitalization.

Example: the Color Purple The Color Purple

1. The mona lisa ______________________

2. The princess and the pea ______________________

3. The boy Who Laughed too much ______________________

4. the Man with One red Shoe ______________________

5. The tempest ______________________

6. Living With Art ______________________

Name ______________________ Date ______________

Vocabulary

Abilities

Use with student book pages 332–333.

play the piano	**cook**	**play chess**
program a computer	**sing**	**draw**
fix a bicycle	**speak Portuguese and Spanish**	

A. Match the sentences with the correct nouns.

Example: Marta can cook	a. a bicycle.
1. Ken can't play	b. a song.
2. Gavin can fix	c. Portuguese.
3. Camilla can't program	d. a computer.
4. Tyler can sing	e. dinner.
5. Mercedes can speak	f. the piano.

B. Complete the dialogues. Use **can, can't,** or the correct verb.

Dialogue 1

Ken: Can you ___cook___?

Marta: No, I (1) ________ cook. But I (2) ________ eat.

Dialogue 2

Camilla: (3) ________ you sing?

Gavin: No, but I (4) ________ play the piano.

Dialogue 3

Tyler: No, I (5) ____ speak Spanish. (6) ____ you?

Mercedes: Yes, I (7) ____.

Dialogue 4

Jack: (8) ________ you (9) ________ a computer?

Terri: Yes, I ________. And I can (10) ________ chess, too.

Name ______________________ Date ______________

Vocabulary

Use with student book pages 334–335.

Problems and Advice
Giving Advice

A. Write the letter of the advice that solves the problem.

Example: My tooth hurts. You should b.

a. put on some sunscreen b. see a dentist

1. I need some information for my report. You should ____.
   a. check the Internet b. call home

2. I have a headache. You should ____.
   a. see a dentist b. take some medicine

3. I lost my cell phone. You should ____.
   a. call for help b. go to the lost-and-found

4. I forgot my books at home. You should ____.
   a. see a doctor b. check your locker

B. Read each sentence. Circle **problem** or **advice** to identify each sentence.

Example: My tooth hurts. **(problem)** **advice**

1. I forgot my workbook at home. **problem** **advice**
2. You should take some medicine. **problem** **advice**
3. She should practice in the computer laboratory. **problem** **advice**
4. He can't find his watch. **problem** **advice**

C. Now state the problem or the advice.

Example: You should see a dentist. I have a toothache.

1. I forgot my workbook at home. ______________________
2. I have a fever that started four days ago. ______________________
3. You should put on some sunscreen. ______________________

Name ______________________ Date ______________

Grammar

Can

Use with student book page 336.

Use **can** to talk about abilities.

Question		
Modal	**Subject**	**Base verb**
Can	I / you / he / she / it / we / they	sing?

Affirmative statement	Negative statement
I can sing.	He can't sing. You cannot sing.

A. Make questions with **can** and the verb phrases in parentheses.

Example: (solve this problem) Can you solve this problem?

1. (play the piano) ______________________
2. (program a computer) ______________________
3. (find his keys) ______________________
4. (cook breakfast) ______________________

B. Read your questions in exercise A. Answer them in the affirmative or negative.

Example: (negative) No, I can't solve this problem.

1. (affirmative) ______________________
2. (negative) ______________________
3. (negative) ______________________
4. (affirmative) ______________________

C. Fix the incorrect sentences. Use **can** or **can't.** Write **correct** if it is correct.

Example: Can I pizza now? Can I eat the pizza now?

1. You ride a bike well? ______________________
2. She speak Chinese. ______________________
3. Can she delicious food? ______________________
4. I can't go to the park today. ______________________

Name ______________________________ Date ____________________

Grammar

Should

Use with student book pages 336–337.

Use **should** to give advice or solutions to problems.

Question		
Modal	**Subject**	**Base verb**
Should	I / you / he / she / it / we / they	tell the teacher?

Affirmative statement	Negative statement
I should study.	He shouldn't get up. You should not get up.

A. Circle the correct word to complete the sentences.

Example: You _____ stay up until 3:00 tomorrow morning. **should** **(shouldn't)**

1. You _____ see a doctor if your leg is broken. **should** **shouldn't**
2. He _____ ask his mother before he goes. **should** **shouldn't**
3. They _____ find more information to do their report. **should** **shouldn't**
4. You _____ play basketball when your foot hurts. **should** **shouldn't**

B. Give advice to a friend. Use **should** or **shouldn't** in your answers.

Example: Should I go to the late movie? No, you shouldn't stay up that late.

1. Should I ride my bike in the snow?

   ____

2. Should I go to school when I am sick?

   ____

3. Should I eat dinner every night?

   ____

4. Should I clean my room?

   ____

5. Should I eat vegetables?

   ____

6. Should I do my homework tonight?

   ____

Name ______________________ Date ______________

Grammar Expansion

Modals: may, might, could

Modals of possibility describe how likely something is to happen. Modals go before verbs.

Modal	Meaning	Example
may	bigger chance for something to happen	He **may** go to the store tonight.
might	smaller chance for something to happen	He **might** play with us today.
could	ability for something to happen	They **could** visit our house.

A. Circle the meaning of each modal.

Example: It **might** rain today. **smaller chance** (circled) **bigger chance** **ability**

1. He **could** help us. **smaller chance** **bigger chance** **ability**
2. He **may** go there. **smaller chance** **bigger chance** **ability**
3. They **might** like it. **smaller chance** **bigger chance** **ability**
4. She **could** do it. **smaller chance** **bigger chance** **ability**
5. Rosa **may** want that. **smaller chance** **bigger chance** **ability**
6. He **might** come. **smaller chance** **bigger chance** **ability**
7. They **could** go. **smaller chance** **bigger chance** **ability**
8. Carla **may** like it. **smaller chance** **bigger chance** **ability**

B. Now make new sentences. Use the modals in parentheses.

Example: (could) We could go to the store tonight.

1. (may) ______________________
2. (could) ______________________
3. (might) ______________________

Name ______________________________ Date ____________________

Word Study

Use with student book page 338.

Vowel: Long e

A. Read each sentence. Circle the words with the long **e** sound.

Example: Let's (eat) the (sweet) (peach).

1. I will eat cheese and meat for lunch.
2. The Greens live on East Beech Street.
3. Please read to us about the mean queen.
4. The sand on the beach feels good on my feet.
5. I will teach you to drive the clean jeep.
6. Here is the key for the screen door.

B. Say the word for each picture. Write **ee, ey,** or **ea** to complete each word.

Example:  b ee

1.  k ____
2.  l ____ f
3.  kn ____
4.  sl ____ p
5.  t ____ m

C. Say the words. Circle the word with a different vowel sound.

Example: beep bead (bird) bee

1. snow sea neat key
2. greet dream six leak
3. teeth clock three seal
4. milk meal sheep speech
5. seen peak flag reef
6. green fed team Pete

Name ______________________ Date ______________

Writing Assignment

Advice Letter

Use with student book page 339.

A. You have a friend who needs advice. Choose which problem you want to write advice about.

1. Your friend is not ready for a test.
2. Your friend is feeling sick.
3. Your friend wants to learn to swim.

B. Make a list of advice to tell your friend. Make short notes.

Example: • find a swimming teacher

- ______________________
- ______________________
- ______________________
- ______________________
- ______________________
- ______________________

C. Now make sentences with your advice. Hint: Use **can** and **should.**

Example: You should find a teacher who can teach you to swim.

____

____

____

____

____

____

____

____

____

Name ______________________ Date ______________

Vocabulary From the Reading

Use with student book page 341.

Key Vocabulary
ability
accident
adopted
invention
tribe

A. Match each Key Vocabulary word with its definition.

Example: __c__ ability — a. accepted or welcomed

1. ____ accident — b. something not planned
2. ____ adopted — ~~c. power to do something~~
3. ____ invention — d. a new thing
4. ____ tribe — e. a community

B. Fill in the blanks with the correct Key Vocabulary word.

Example: The construction company ____adopted____ the engineer's new plan.

1. He has the ______________ to be a professional pianist.
2. The ______________ of the new machine made the workers' job much easier.
3. Navajos are a ______________ of people who live in Arizona.
4. I didn't want the glass to break. It was an ______________.

C. Practice using the Key Vocabulary words. Make sentences with the words in parentheses.

Example: (adopted) Once everyone agreed, the new club rule was adopted.

1. (ability) ______________________________
2. (accident) ______________________________
3. (tribe) ______________________________
4. (invention) ______________________________

Name ______________________ Date ______________________

Reading Strategy

Use with student book page 342.

Summarize

When you summarize something, you make it shorter. You only give the important ideas. First, look at the topic sentence to find the main idea. Then look through the text for other important details.

Academic Vocabulary for the Reading Strategy		
Word	**Explanation**	**Sample Sentence**
summarize	give the main points of a story or article	I don't have time to read the whole report. Can you **summarize** it for me?
topic sentence	a sentence that gives the main idea of a paragraph	The **topic sentence** is usually the first sentence in a paragraph.

A. Read this text from Unit 4.

How to Make a Perfect Sandwich

There are many things you need to make the perfect sandwich. First, you must start with good bread. Make sure the pieces of bread aren't too thick. Next, put on a condiment such as mustard or mayonnaise. Don't put on too much. Tomato and lettuce are important because they are healthy. You also need protein. Don't forget to put on your favorite meat or cheese!

Now answer the questions.

Example: What is the title of this paragraph? How to Make a Perfect Sandwich

1. What is the topic sentence of this paragraph? ______________________

____

2. Summarize the information about bread. ______________________

____

3. Summarize the information about condiments. ______________________

____

4. Summarize the last two sentences. ______________________

____

Name ______________________________ Date ____________________

Text Genre
Biography

Use with student book page 342.

A biography is about another person. It gives important information about events and actions in that person's life.

Biography	
events	things that happen in a person's life
actions	things a person does
dates	when things happen in a person's life
sequence	the order that things happen

Read the text.

Carl Sagan

Carl Sagan was born in New York in 1934. He graduated from high school in 1951. He was interested in a kind of science called astronomy. Astronomy is the study of stars. Carl Sagan taught astronomy at colleges. He also helped build ships to fly into space. In 1980, he made a science TV show called *Cosmos: A Personal Voyage*. This TV show was played in more than 60 countries. Carl Sagan was a very important scientist.*

* a scientist is someone who studies science

Now answer the questions.

Example: What is a scientist? A scientist is someone who studies science.

1. Name one event that happened in Carl Sagan's life.

____

2. Name one action he did.

____

3. Show the sequence of events. Put numbers next to each event.

_______ He also helped build ships to fly into space.

_______ In 1980, he made a science TV show.

_______ Carl Sagan taught astronomy at colleges.

___1___ Carl Sagan was born in New York in 1934.

_______ He graduated from high school in 1951.

Name ______________________ Date ______________

Reading Comprehension

Use with student book page 348.

A. Choose the correct answer. Write the letter in the blank.

Example: __a__ When was the first Cherokee newspaper printed in the U.S.?

a. 1828 b. 1776 c. 1912

1. ____ When was Sequoyah born?
   a. 1828 b. 1776 c. 1912

2. ____ In what state was Sequoyah born?
   a. Mississippi b. Oklahoma c. Tennessee

3. ____ What did Sequoyah do before his accident?
   a. fur trader b. shoemaker c. doctor

4. ____ What did Sequoyah become after his accident?
   a. doctor b. firefighter c. silversmith

5. ____ What did the Cherokee mean when they said "talking leaves"?
   a. money b. paper c. gods

B. Summarize the topics.

1. Summarize the information about Sequoyah's parents.

   ____

   ____

2. Summarize what Sequoyah invented.

   ____

   ____

3. Summarize how people thought about what Sequoyah invented.

   ____

   ____

Name ______________________ Date ______________

Text Element

Use with student book page 349.

Figurative Language: Metaphors

Words with **figurative language** don't have their regular meaning. Metaphors are one kind of figurative language. A **metaphor** describes one thing by comparing it with another thing.

A. Read the sentences. Circle **metaphor** if the sentence contains a metaphor. If it doesn't, circle **not a metaphor.**

Example: He was a bull in a china shop. (**metaphor**) **not a metaphor**

1. She was as happy as a pig in mud. **metaphor** **not a metaphor**
2. They saw the angry dog. **metaphor** **not a metaphor**
3. She smiled at me. **metaphor** **not a metaphor**
4. We are floating on a cloud. **metaphor** **not a metaphor**

B. What two things are being compared? Use adjectives and adverbs.

Example: He was a bull in a china shop. a clumsy man and a clumsy bull

1. The hungry students flew to the cafeteria. ______________
2. He was boiling mad at the other driver. ______________
3. She is a teddy bear. ______________
4. The lake is a bright mirror. ______________
5. His teeth are snow white. ______________

C. Make a sentence with a metaphor. Use the words in parentheses ( ).

Example: (she / teddy bear) She is a teddy bear.

1. (his smile / the morning sun) ______________
2. (her face / red balloon) ______________
3. (her eyes / bright stars) ______________

Name ______________________ Date ______________

Vocabulary

Use with student book pages 364–365.

Places in the Community

bookstore	**community center**	**music store**	**restaurant**
clothing store	**movie theater**	**park**	**shopping mall**

A. Write the vocabulary item for each picture.

movie theater

1. ______________

2. ______________

3. ______________

4. ______________

5. ______________

B. Look at the map.

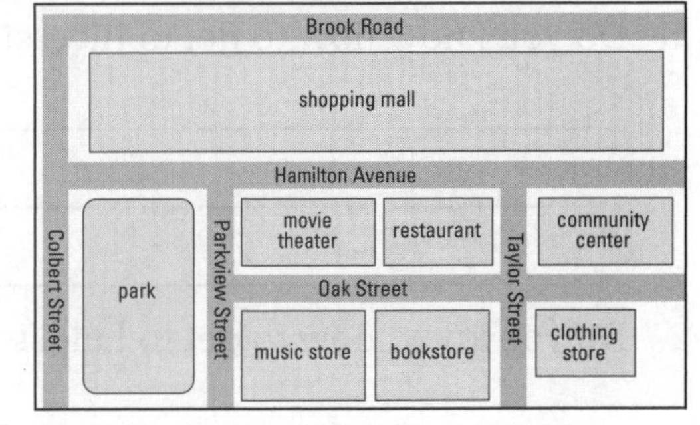

Fill in the blanks with **across from, between, beside, on,** or **on the corner of.**

Example: The shopping mall is across from the movie theater.

1. The movie theater is ______________ Hamilton Avenue and Parkview Street.
2. The shopping mall is ______________ Brook Road.
3. The park is ______________ Colbert Street and Parkview Street.
4. The restaurant is ______________ the bookstore.
5. The bookstore is ______________ the music store.

Name ______________________ Date ______________

Vocabulary

Use with student book pages 366–367.

Giving Directions

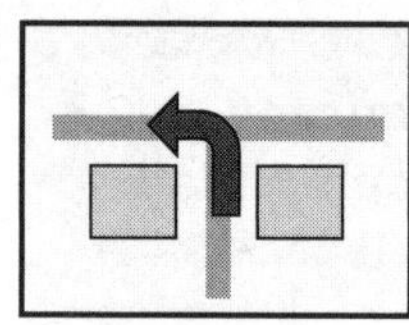
turn left

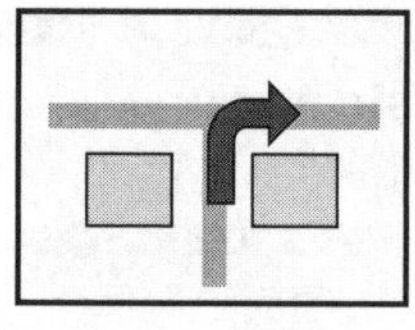
turn right

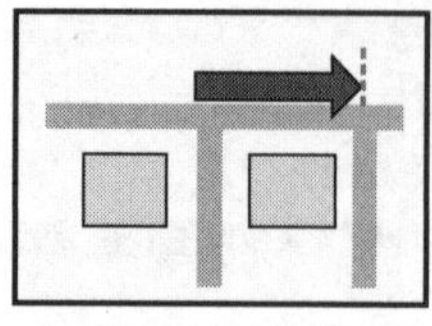
walk one block

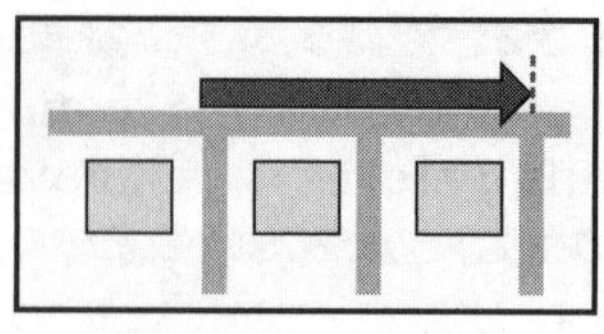
go straight two blocks

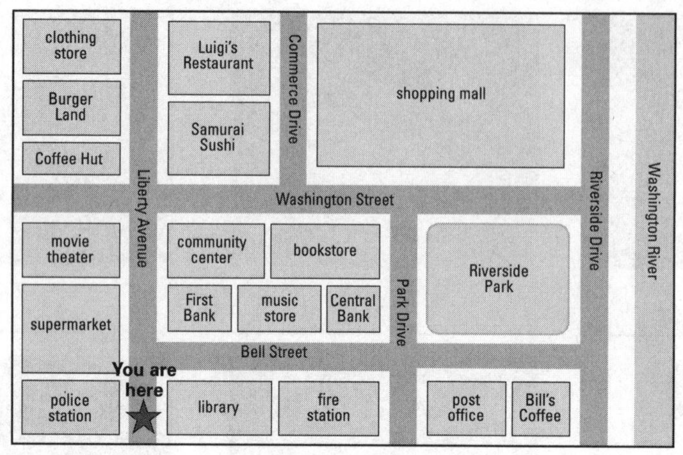

Give directions.

Example: Do you know how to get to the shopping mall?

Go straight two blocks on Liberty Avenue. Turn right onto Washington Street. Go one block to Commerce Drive. The shopping mall is on your left.

1. Do you know how to get to Riverside Park?

____

____

____

2. Do you know how to get to Luigi's Restaurant?

____

____

____

3. Do you know how to get to Central Bank?

____

____

____

Name ______________________ Date ______________

Grammar

Comparative Adjectives

Use with student book pages 368–369.

Use **comparative adjectives** to compare two things. Use a comparative adjective and **than** when talking about both things in the same sentence.

1. Add **er** to the end of most adjectives.
2. For adjectives that end in **e**, add **r**.
3. For one-syllable adjectives that end in a vowel + a consonant, double the consonant and add **er**.
4. For adjectives that end in **y**, change the **y** to **i** and add **er**.

A. Change the adjective in parentheses into a comparative adjective.

Example: The dog is faster than the boy. (fast)

1. The pencil is ______________ than the notebook. (cheap)
2. This jacket is ______________ than that one. (nice)
3. Arizona is ______________ than Vermont. (hot)
4. My father is ______________ than my uncle. (big)
5. His sister is ______________ than him. (old)
6. This movie is ______________ than the movie I saw last weekend. (funny)

B. Put the words in the correct order.

Example: (The / the / is / than / faster / dog / boy.)

The dog is faster than the boy.

1. (was / than / last / The / simpler / test / this / test.)

____

2. (homework. / homework / than / harder / is / yesterday's / Today's)

____

3. (story. / story / than / sadder / This / the / other / is)

____

4. (than / scarf / The / scarf. / shorter / blue / the / purple / is)

____

Name ______________________ Date ______________

For most adjectives with two syllables, and all adjectives with three or more syllables, use **more** in front of the adjective. A few adjectives are irregular.

C. Unscramble the letters of the comparative adjectives in parentheses. Write them on the lines.

Example: My bag is better than that one. (tteerb)

1. This movie is ______________ than that one. (riarces)
2. This water is ______________ than that water. (lodcer)
3. Her mother is ______________ than her father. (relalt)
4. The red car is more ______________ than the yellow car. (evisnepex)

D. Change the adjectives in parentheses into comparative adjectives.

Example: A lion is more dangerous than a cat. (dangerous)

1. Vegetables are ______________ than bread. (healthy)
2. The boots are ______________ than the umbrella. (expensive)
3. Homework is ______________ than a pep rally. (important)
4. These grapes are ______________ than last week's grapes. (bad)
5. The sunset is ______________ than the rain. (beautiful)

E. Make sentences that compare the two nouns in parentheses. Use at least two comparative adjectives that use the word **more**.

Example: (lion / cat) A lion is more dangerous than a cat.

1. (river / ocean) ______________
2. (plane / car) ______________
3. (teacher / firefighter) ______________
4. (stethoscope / scissors) ______________
5. (grasshopper / wolf) ______________

Name ______________________ Date ______________

Grammar Expansion

Comparative Adverbs

To make **comparative adverbs,** use *more* in front of the adverb and *than* before the object.

The blue pen writes **more smoothly than** the black pen.

The dog plays **more happily** today **than** it did yesterday.

A. Change each adjective in parentheses into a comparative adverb.

Example: The football team runs more quickly than they did last year. (quick)

1. You should eat a watermelon ______________ than you eat a banana. (careful)
2. I eat ______________ than he does. (slow)
3. She acts ______________ when she is happy than when she is angry. (nice)
4. Ms. Lopez teaches ______________ than Mr. Miller does. (patient)
5. He works ______________ now than he did before. (successful)

B. Write sentences with comparative adverbs. Use the words in parentheses.

Example: (Mr. Garcia / Maria / talk / loud)

Mr. Garcia talks more loudly than Maria.

1. (He / she / run / slow)

____

2. (Julio / Fernando / eat / quick)

____

3. (boy / man / play / happy)

____

4. (Clara / Tom / sing / beautiful)

____

5. (Joe / Elizabeth / smile / wide)

____

Name ______________________ Date ______________

Word Study

Use with student book page 370.

Diphthongs: oi and oy

A. Say the word for the picture. Write the word with the same vowel sound.

Example: Roy barn look Roy

1. sleep joy rose ________
2. cube tail broil ________
3. loyal tray snow ________
4. crab point smile ________
5. spoon voice milk ________
6. shelf enjoy plate ________

B. Write **oi** or **oy** to finish each word.

Example: R oy made n oi se with his t oy drum.

1. B ____ l the water in the big pot and br ____ l the meat in the oven.
2. I'll trade this old c ____ n for your new t ____.
3. Put some ____ l on the pasta to keep it m ____ st.
4. P ____ nt to the b ____ who made the loud n ____ se.
5. I enj ____ eating s ____ beans in my salad.

C. Divide the words into beginning, middle, and end sounds. Keep the letters in the diphthong together.

Example: coin c / oi / n

1. oil ________
2. toy ________
3. soy ________
4. soil ________
5. boil ________
6. joy ________

Name ______________________ Date ______________

Word Study

Suffixes: ful, able, ish
Suffixes: ion, ous, ness

Use with student book pages 371–372.

Suffixes: ful, less, able, ish	
Suffix	**Meaning**
ful	full of
less	without
able	can be done
ish	like, in the same way as

Suffixes: ion, ous, ness	
Suffix	**Parts of Speech**
ion	verbs → nouns
ous	nouns → adjectives
ness	adjectives → nouns

A. Write the correct word. Use the suffixes: **ful, les, able,** and **ish.**

Example: with care c a r e f u l

1. without hope __ __ __ __ __ __ __ __
2. like a child __ __ __ __ __ __ __ __
3. can be washed __ __ __ __ __ __ __ __
4. full of color __ __ __ __ __ __ __ __
5. without sun __ __ __ __ __ __ __
6. the same way as a baby __ __ __ __ __ __ __

B. Read the sentences and look at the underlined words. Write the missing words on the lines. Use the suffixes: **ion, ous,** or **ness.**

Example: He has much fame. He is famous.

1. He has a lot of courage. He is ______________.
2. The principal will present an award during the ______________ tomorrow.
3. If you want to reserve the room, make a ______________ for it.
4. She is kind. She always shows ______________.

Name ________________________ Date ____________

Writing Assignment

Personal Narrative

Use with student book page 373.

How is your life different now than it was five years ago?

A. Make a list of important activities.

School Activities Now

Example: study for science tests	

School Activities Five Years Ago

Example: study for spelling tests	

After-School Activities Now

Example: e-mail friends	

After-School Activities Five Years Ago

Example: ride my bicycle	

B. Look at your school and after-school activities. Make comparative sentences. Use comparative adjectives and comparative adverbs.

Example: I work harder in school now than I did five years ago. Spelling was harder than science. Now I study for science more seriously than I do for spelling.

Name ______________________ Date ______________

Vocabulary From the Reading

Use with student book page 375.

Key Vocabulary

barn	field	net
beak	grain	stream

A. Match the Key Vocabulary word with the definitions.

Example: __b__ barn
1. ____ beak
2. ____ field
3. ____ grain
4. ____ net
5. ____ stream

a. a kind of food like rice, corn, or wheat
~~b. a building on a farm~~
c. a bird's mouth
d. a small river
e. a place where farmers grow things
f. something used to catch animals

B. Complete each sentence with the correct Key Vocabulary word.

Example: The bird has a sharp __beak__.

1. The fisherman catches fish in his ______________.
2. My favorite kind of ______________ is rice.
3. The farmer grows corn in this ______________.
4. He drank water from the cold ______________.
5. The farmer keeps hay in the red ______________.

C. Make sentences with the words in parentheses.

Example: (beak) The bird had a worm in its beak.

1. (field) ______________
2. (net) ______________
3. (stream) ______________
4. (barn) ______________
5. (grain) ______________

Name ______________________ Date ______________

Reading Strategy

Understand Characters

Use with student book page 376.

To **understand characters**, you see how their **motives** explain their **traits.**

Academic Vocabulary for Reading Strategy		
Word	**Explanation**	**Sample Sentence**
trait	characteristic or quality that someone has	The main character has good **traits.** She is hardworking and kind.
motive	reason for doing something	Ted's **motive** for eating was he was hungry.

A. Identify the motives and traits. Write **motive** or **trait.**

Example: trait The worker was always punctual.

1. ______________ They didn't want to cook. They went to a restaurant.
2. ______________ He used the flashlight to see.
3. ______________ The car is reliable in bad weather.
4. ______________ The students were tired so they were quiet.

B. Read the story.

Jim was a hardworking student. Father was loving. He wanted Jim to do well. He said, "If you do well on this test, we can go to the movies." Jim did well on the test. Father told Jim he was very proud. That night, they went to the movies.

Answer the questions.

Example: What trait does Jim have? He is a hardworking student.

1. What trait does Jim's father have? ______________
2. What did Father say to Jim? ______________
____
3. What was Father's motive for saying that to Jim?
____
____

Name ______________________ Date ______________

Text Genre

Use with student book page 376.

Folktales and Fables

Folktales and **fables** are types of traditional stories. A folktale is a timeless story that is usually passed on orally among a group of people. A fable is usually a story with animals as the **characters.** There is often a lesson in these stories. This lesson, or message, is a **moral.**

Folktales and Fables	
characters	people, or animals, in a story
moral	a message, or a lesson, that you can learn from the story

Read the story.

The Ant and the Grasshopper

Every year the cornfield got cold in the winter. When the field got cold, the animals couldn't find food. They saved food during the warm months. Then they ate the food during the cold months. One summer day, an ant and a grasshopper were in the cornfield. The grasshopper wanted to play and sing and sleep. The ant wanted to find food to save for winter. Later, winter came. The grasshopper was cold and hungry. He went to the ant's house. The ant smiled and told the grasshopper to come inside with her and eat. When spring came, the ant and the grasshopper started to gather food for the next winter together.

Answer the questions.

Example: What is the title of the story?

The Ant and the Grasshopper

1. Who are the characters in the story?

____

2. What are the ant's character traits?

____

3. What are the grasshopper's character traits?

____

4. Is this a folktale or a fable? How do you know?

____

Name ______________________________ Date ____________________

Reading Comprehension

Use with student book page 382.

A. Answer the questions about "Real Brotherly Love."

Example: __a__ What country is the folktale from?

a. Korea b. China c. Egypt

1. _____ What is the brothers' occupation?

a. farmer b. baker c. teacher

2. _____ Where did the brothers keep their grain?

a. in the house b. in a barn c. outside

3. _____ What happened to the grain Older Brother gave to Younger Brother?

a. He lost it. b. Mice ate it. c. Younger Brother returned it.

B. Answer the questions about "The Ant and the Dove."

Example: Who is the author? __b__

a. Ben Franklin b. Aesop c. Rosa Parks

1. What did the ant fall into? _____

a. a net b. a stream c. a barn

2. What did the dove give to the ant? _____

a. a leaf b. piece of wood c. grain of rice

3. How did the ant help the dove? _____

a. He called to him. b. He ate the net. c. He bit the birdcatcher.

C. Think about the traits of Younger Brother, Older Brother, the ant, and the dove. What trait do they all have?

____

____

____

Name ______________________ Date ______________

Literary Element

Moral

Use with student book page 383.

A **moral** is a lesson or message in a story.

Read the story.

The Lion's Only Fear

There once was a lion who feared only one thing. He feared the sound of a chicken. One day, he told an elephant about his fear. The elephant laughed. "How can a chicken hurt a lion?" asked the elephant. Then a mouse ran by and the elephant jumped in fear of it. "Don't let it get near me!" the elephant screamed. Now it was the lion's turn to laugh.

Answer the questions.

Example: What is the title of the story?

The Lion's Only Fear

1. Who are the main characters in the story?

____

____

____

2. What is the moral of the story?

____

____

____

____

____

____

Name ______________________________ Date ____________________

Writing Conventions

Use with student book page 383.

Punctuation: Parentheses and Commas

Parentheses and **commas** give extra information or an explanation in a reading. Sometimes you can use commas instead of parentheses. Here are some examples:

"The Ant and the Dove" (by Aesop) is a famous fable.

"The Ant and the Dove," by Aesop, is a famous fable.

A. Circle **correct** for the correct sentences and **incorrect** for the incorrect sentences.

Example: My sister, Juanita, likes this book. (correct) incorrect

1. The story (the one you don't like) is my favorite. correct incorrect
2. The book called *Milestones,* also has a workbook. correct incorrect
3. The man the one over there is my uncle. correct incorrect
4. The new computer (my computer) is very good. correct incorrect
5. This bread made by my friend) is delicious. correct incorrect

B. Put a comma (,) before and after extra information.

Example: The book**,** the yellow book, is really good.

1. The sun the summer sun is very hot.
2. The car the one over there is ours.
3. The dog sleeping in the yard is very friendly.
4. The barn the red barn is new.

C. Put parentheses ( ) before and after extra information.

Example: My thesaurus (by Roget) is easy to use.

1. I eat vegetables like tomatoes, spinach, and broccoli with every meal.
2. Large rivers such as the Mississippi and the Nile have streams around them.
3. Most farm animals chickens, cows, and pigs eat grain or hay.
4. That painting *The View of Toledo* was painted by El Greco.
5. Mr. Miller my favorite teacher is in Room 104.
6. That basketball the one on the shelf is Mario's.

Name ______________________ Date ______________

Vocabulary

Neighborhood Places

Use with student book pages 388–389.

bank	**gas station**	**library**	**post office**
convenience store	**laundromat**	**pharmacy**	

A. Match the place with the action.

Example: __a__ bank — ~~a. keep money safe~~

1. ____ convenience store — b. pick up some bandages
2. ____ gas station — c. buy some water
3. ____ laundromat — d. wash some clothes
4. ____ library — e. return some books
5. ____ pharmacy — f. buy some gasoline
6. ____ post office — g. buy some stamps

B. Fill in the blanks with the correct vocabulary items.

Example: I'm going to the __convenience store__ because we need bread and milk.

1. Ceasar is going to the ____________ because he needs to borrow some books.
2. Ya-Ting and Amanda are going to the ____________ because they need to mail some packages.
3. We have no clean clothes. We must go to the ____________.
4. They have a lot of money in the ____________.
5. He went to the ____________ because he wanted to put air in his bicycle tires.
6. I'm going to the ____________ because the baby needs some cough medicine.

C. Give reasons why you need to go places. Make sentences with *because* and the vocabulary items in parentheses.

Example: (bank) __I have to go to the bank because I need to get some money.__

1. (library) ____________
2. (convenience store) ____________
3. (pharmacy) ____________

Name ______________________ Date ____________

Vocabulary

Famous Places and Attractions

Use with student book pages 390–391.

Great Wall of China	**Pyramids**
Miami Beach	**safari**
Mona Lisa	**Statue of Liberty**

A. Match the attractions with the places.

Example: __f__ Great Wall of China

1. _____ Miami Beach
2. _____ *Mona Lisa*
3. _____ Pyramids
4. _____ safari
5. _____ Statue of Liberty

a. Egypt
b. France
c. Florida
d. Kenya
e. New York
~~f. China~~

B. Complete the sentences. Use the words **Miami Beach, *Mona Lisa*, Pyramids, safari,** or **Statue of Liberty.**

Example: I like nature. I would like to go on a ___safari___.

1. I like to swim. I would like to go to ____________.
2. I like history. I would like to go to the ____________.
3. I like art. I would like to see the ____________.

C. Choose four places from the list and write a sentence about why you would like to go there.

India	Chile	New York	Alaska	Italy	China	New Orleans	Australia

Example: I would like to go to New Orleans to listen to jazz music.

1. ______________________________
2. ______________________________
3. ______________________________
4. ______________________________

Name ______________________ Date ______________

Grammar

Use with student book page 392.

Superlative Adjectives

Use **superlative adjectives** to compare more than two things. Always use **the** before a superlative adjective. For most one-syllable or two-syllable adjectives, add the suffix **-est.** For most adjectives with two or more syllables, use the words **the most** in front of the adjective.

Forming Superlative Adjectives with -est	
tall ➔ the tall**est**	add **est**
nice ➔ the nic**est**	ends in **e**; add **st**
pretty ➔ the pretti**est**	ends in **y**; change to **i** and add **est**
hot ➔ the hot**test**	for single syllable words that end in consonant-vowel-consonant; **double** the last consonant and add **est**

Forming Superlative Adjectives with Most	
interesting ➔	This is **the most interesting** museum in the city.
important ➔	The capitol building is **the most important** building in the city.

A. Change the adjectives in parentheses into superlative adjectives. Use **-est.**

Example: The Nile is ___the longest___ river in the world. (long)

1. Ayaka's grandmother is ______________ person in the family. (nice)
2. Ayaka is ______________ eater in the family. (slow)
3. Ayaka and her twin sister are ______________ in age. (close)
4. Her older brother talks ______________ in the family. (loud)
5. Her Aunt Shizue is ______________ person in the family. (rich)

B. Change the adjectives in parentheses into superlative adjectives. Use **the most.**

Example: The Nile is ___the most dangerous___ river in the world. (dangerous)

1. Yang's father is ______________ person in the family. (patient)
2. His Uncle Li is ______________ person in the family. (successful)
3. Yang's bird is ______________ of his animals. (beautiful)
4. His grandfather is ______________ person in the family. (difficult)
5. Yang is ______________ person in the family. (humorous)

Name ______________________ Date ______________

C. Write sentences about your family. Use superlative adjectives with **-est** or **most.**

Example: (-est, tall) My uncle is the tallest person in my family.

1. (-est, short) ______________________
2. (-est, old) ______________________
3. (most, beautiful) ______________________
4. (most, exciting) ______________________

D. Read the three sentences in each item. Make a sentence with a superlative adjective that summarizes the sentences. Use the adjective in parentheses.

Example: (old) Pam is 18. Karen is 15. Scott is 22. Scott is the oldest.

1. (good) Today's movie was boring. Yesterday's movie was OK. Last week's movie was exciting. ______________________
2. (heavy) Bill weighs 85 pounds. Jon weighs 90 pounds. Mark weighs 92 pounds. ______________________
3. (delicious) Aunt Tanya's food was bad. Aunt Tamisha's food was good. Aunt Tamara's food was very good. ______________________

E. Write three sentences about yourself. Change the adjectives in the first box to the superlative form. Use phrases from the second box.

excited	happy	bored
hungry	relaxed	tired
worried		

at school	during class	during recess
at home	before lunch	before a test
in my room	after class	after gym class

Examples: I am happiest in my room.

I am most hungry after class.

1. ______________________
2. ______________________
3. ______________________

Name ______________________ Date ______________

Grammar Expansion

Superlative Adverbs

To make **superlative adverbs,** use **the most** in front of the adverb.

This pen writes **the most smoothly.**
The bird sings **the most happily** when it is out of its cage.

A. Change the adjective in parentheses into a superlative adverb.

Example: This kind of bread is the most quickly made. (quick)

1. These children are ______________ behaved. (nice)
2. This shirt is ______________ priced. (expensive)
3. This homework assignment was ______________ done. (quick)
4. This test problem was ______________ answered. (poor)

B. Tell if the sentences are correct. Write **correct** or **incorrect.**

Example: correct Our class was the most well prepared.

1. ______________ I can do my homework the most easily after school.
2. ______________ We should talk most quietly in the library.
3. ______________ The most poorly written essays got the lowest grades.
4. ______________ The most patiently waiting students got their rewards first.
5. ______________ The carefully done math homework is usually correct.

C. Now make sentences with superlative adverbs. Use the words in parentheses to help you.

Example: (talk / quiet) My family talks the most quietly at night.

1. (talk / loud) ______________
2. (sleep / deep) ______________
3. (behave / polite) ______________

Name ______________________ Date ______________

Word Study

Use with student book page 394.

Diphthongs: ow, ou for /ow/
Phonemic Awareness

A. Say the word for the picture. Write the correct spelling of the word.

Example:  cou cow cow

3.  house howse ________

1.  couch cowch ________

4.  toun town ________

2.  flouer flower ________

5. 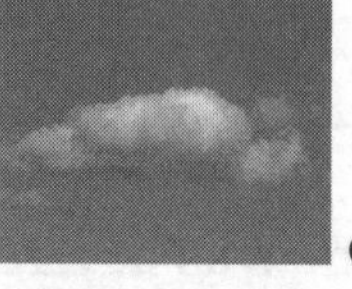 cloud clowd ________

B. Circle the words in each sentence that have the **ow** sound. Then write the words in the chart where they belong.

Example: The (brown) (owl) caught the (mouse).

1. The loud clown made me frown.
2. The hound made a howling sound at the crowd.
3. I am proud of how we cleaned the house.
4. The round tower almost touched the clouds.
5. Your gown is about to touch the ground.

ou		ow	
mouse		brown	owl

Name ______________________ Date ______________

Writing Assignment

Descriptive Essay

Use with student book page 395.

A. Think about the best or worst place you ever visited. Then answer the questions.

Example: What was the weather like? It was very cold and it rained a lot.

1. What is the name of the place? ______________________
2. When did you go? ______________________
3. How did you get there? ______________________
4. Who went with you? ______________________
5. Why did you go there? ______________________
6. What was the weather like? ______________________

B. List three comparative and superlative adjectives to make your writing more interesting.

Comparative Adjectives	Superlative Adjectives
Example: more rain than usual	Example: the most stars I ever saw

Name ______________________ Date ______________

Vocabulary From the Reading

Use with student book page 397.

Key Vocabulary

allowed	document
amendment	vote
approve	war

A. Match the Key Vocabulary word with the correct definition.

Example: c allowed — a. allow something to happen

1. ____ amendment — b. official paper
2. ____ approve — ~~c. being able to do something~~
3. ____ document — d. countries or people fight each other
4. ____ vote — e. what you do to elect someone or something
5. ____ war — f. a change of a plan or law

B. Fill in the crossword puzzle. Complete the sentences. Put the answers in the correct boxes.

ACROSS

1. After we made the amendment, the company was happy with the plan.
2. The two countries are at ____________. When will the fighting end?
3. A passport is an example of a ____________.

DOWN

4. We are not ____________ to enter. The gate is locked.
5. My parents ____________ my decision.
6. Did you ____________ for class president?

Name ______________________ Date ______________

Reading Strategy

Use with student book page 398.

Identify the Author's Purpose and Audience

To **identify the author's purpose and audience** means to find out why and for whom someone wrote something.

Academic Vocabulary for the Reading Strategy		
Word	**Explanation**	**Sample Sentence**
inform	to give information or facts to someone	The principal **informed** the students there was a school concert on Thursday.
audience	a person or people who read something an author has written	The **audience** for this book is teenagers, but adults like to read it too.

A. Circle the author's purpose.

Example: notes taken in history class **entertain** **(inform)** **persuade**

1. telephone book **entertain** **inform** **persuade**
2. comic book **entertain** **inform** **persuade**
3. essay on the importance of recycling **entertain** **inform** **persuade**
4. calendar **entertain** **inform** **persuade**
5. history textbook **entertain** **inform** **persuade**
6. directions on how to build a desk **entertain** **inform** **persuade**
7. dictionary **entertain** **inform** **persuade**

B. Identify the audience.

Example: notes taken in history class student

1. telephone book ______________________
2. comic book ______________________
3. essay on the importance of recycling ______________________
4. calendar ______________________
5. history textbook ______________________
6. directions on how to build a desk ______________________
7. dictionary ______________________

Name ______________________ Date ______________

Text Genre

Use with student book page 398.

Informational Text: Textbook

Textbooks give information. Textbooks have many features to help explain information.

Textbook	
title	the name of a chapter or text
heading	the name of a part of the text
time line	a graphic that shows when things happen
maps	illustrations that show where things happen
index	a list that shows where to find specific words or topics

A. Circle which textbook element you would use to find out what you want to know.

Example: where something happened (**map**) **index** **time line**

1. what page something is on **map** **index** **time line**
2. when something happened **map** **index** **time line**
3. when someone lived **map** **index** **time line**
4. where someone went **map** **index** **time line**

B. Write the textbook element needed to answer the question.

Example: What pages tell about the U.S. Constitution?

Look in the index.

1. Where is Washington D.C.?

____

2. When did the Civil War happen?

____

3. What page tells about Rosa Parks?

____

4. How long did Benjamin Franklin live?

____

5. Where did the Revolutionary War happen?

____

Name ______________________ Date ______________

Reading Comprehension

Use with student book page 404.

A. Choose the correct letter to answer the questions.

Example: ___b___ As of 2007, how many amendments were there?

a. 10 b. 27 c. 200

1. ________ When was the Constitution written?

a. 1963 b. 1787 c. 1521

2. ________ Which of these is a right in the Bill of Rights?

a. free speech b. have slaves c. go to bed late

3. ________ What did the 15th amendment do?

a. It guaranteed free speech. b. It declared war with France. c. It gave African Americans the right to vote.

4. ________ What did the Framers make?

a. nothing b. picture frames c. the U.S. Constitution

B. Answer the questions.

1. What is the Bill of Rights? ______________________

____

2. What are the three branches of the U.S. government?

__________ __________ __________

3. What is the purpose of each branch of government?

- ______________________

  ____
- ______________________

  ____
- ______________________

  ____

Name ______________________ Date ______________

Text Element

Use with student book page 405.

Index

Textbooks usually have an index in the back of the book. An index lists page numbers where specific information can be found. Topics are listed in alphabetical order by key words or phrases.

Use the index to answer the questions.

Example: What kind of information is on pages 557–559?
The U.S. Supreme Court

1. Where can you find information on the U.S. Congress?
____

2. What kind of information is on pages 188–197?
____

3. Where can you find details about the Civil Rights Movement?
____

4. Where can you find information on the Continental Congress?
____

5. What kind of information is on pages 120–135?
____

6. What kind of information is on pages 491–495?
____

Name ______________________________ Date ______________

Vocabulary

Shopping for Clothing

Use with student book pages 420–421.

aisle	dress	label	shelf	size	tie
belt	hanger	pants	shirt	skirt	
blouse	jeans	rack	shopping cart	sweater	

A. Write the vocabulary in the correct places on the pictures.

B. Complete the conversation by filling in the blanks. Use the words below.

~~help~~	Men's	Women's	label	aisle	shopping cart	shelf

Example: Can I ______help______ you? Yes, please.

1. Where are the ties? They are in the ______________ Department.
2. Where are the belts? They are in ______________ 4.
3. Where are the dresses? They are in the ______________ Department.
4. What do you want to buy? I have two shirts in my ______________.
5. What size is this sweater? Did you look at the ______________?
6. Where are the jeans? They are on the bottom ______________.

Name ____________________ Date ____________

Vocabulary

Use with student book pages 422–423.

Questions and Answers for Shopping

Statements	Questions
This looks too big.	Where can I try it on?
This is too small.	Do you have it in a smaller size?
I don't like this color.	Do you have it in another color?
This is too small.	Do you have this in a medium?
This is too large.	Can I return it?
The label says "dry clean only."	Can I hand wash it?

A. Read the statement. Then circle the letter of the correct question that follows it.

Example: I like this dress.
ⓐ Where can I try it on?
b. Where is the men's department?

1. This shirt is blue.
   a. Do you have this in another color?
   b. Do you have this in a smaller size?

2. This shirt is too big.
   a. Where is the Men's Department?
   b. Can I return it?

3. This medium shirt is too small.
   a. Do you have a large?
   b. Do you have this in another color?

4. I need a smaller shoe.
   a. Do you have a size 7?
   b. Do you have any dresses?

B. Complete the conversations. Use the words and phrases below.

~~hand wash~~	too big	take it	try this on	another size	another color	return

Example: Can I __hand wash__ these pants? Yes, you can dry clean them, too.

1. Excuse me. Can I ____________ this shirt? Of course. What's the problem?

2. Would you like to buy this skirt? Yes, I'll ____________.

3. Where can I ____________? In the fitting room.

4. These shoes don't fit. They're ____________.

5. Do you like this black sweater? No. Do you have it in ____________?

6. This blouse is too big. Do you have it in ____________?

Name ______________________ Date ______________

Grammar

Use with student book pages 424–425.

Using Will to Talk About the Future

Using Will to Talk About the Future	
Affirmative	**Negative**
I **will** run.	I **will not** walk.
He **will** dance.	He **will not** sing.
We **will** study.	We **will not** watch TV.
They **will** shop.	They **will not** pay later.

Yes / No Questions with Will			Short Answers with Will
Will	I/you he/she/it we/they	shop?	Yes, he will. No, you won't.

A. Put the verbs in parentheses in the future tense with **will.**

Example: I will run tomorrow morning. (run)

1. Miguel ______________ at the school dance. (dance)
2. Ya-Ting ______________ to school. (walk)
3. Jeff and Sandra ______________ for a gift. (shop)
4. We ______________ lettuce, tomatoes, and carrots to make a salad. (buy)

B. Answer the questions with the subject + **will** or **won't.**

Example: Will you run in the morning? No, I won't.

1. Will they study after dinner? Yes, ______________.
2. Will you walk to the shopping mall? No, ______________.
3. Will he sing in the school concert? Yes, ______________.
4. Will it rain later? No, ______________.
5. Will you bring some cookies to my party? Yes, ______________.

Name ______________________ Date ______________

C. Complete the questions with nouns or pronouns and the verbs in parentheses. Remember to use **will** in your question.

Example: Who will you see at the mall? (you / see)

1. What ______________ after graduation? (Luis / do)
2. When ______________ to bed? (the children / go)
3. Who ______________ to your party? (you / invite)
4. Where ______________ to next year? (they / move)
5. Why ______________ so early? (Janet / leave)
6. How ______________ that heavy bed? (she / lift)

D. Put the words in the correct order to ask **wh-** questions with **will.**

Example: (see / will / Who / mall? / at / the / you) Who will you see at the mall?

1. (Who / first? / go / will) ______________
2. (to / What / he / say / will / them?) ______________
3. (over? / this / When / test / be / will) ______________
4. (Where / find / keys? / will / her / she) ______________
5. (be / will / sale? / it / on / Why) ______________
6. (How / no / they / car? / there / with / will / get) ______________

E. Write **yes/no** questions using **will** and the verbs in parentheses. Then answer the questions in the affirmative and the negative.

Example: (run) Will you run in the morning? Yes, I will. No, I won't.

1. (sleep) ______________
2. (go) ______________
3. (play) ______________

Name ______________________ Date ______________

Grammar Expansion

More Wh- Questions with Will

To make yes/no questions with **will**, use **will** before the subject and verb. Answer with **will** or **won't**.

Wh- Questions with Will	
Who will I see at the mall?	You will see Jim and Pat.
What will you get?	I will get some shoes.
Where will he go shopping?	He will go to the mall.
When will she try it on?	She will try it on tonight.
How will we know if our shoes fit?	We will try them on.
Why will they return it?	They will return it because it's too small.

A. Ask a **wh-** question with **will** to get the response.

Example: (when) He will go home at 4 P.M. When will he go home?

1. (who) She will go to the school dance with Raul. ______
2. (where) He will go to Mexico for his vacation. ______
3. (what) He will play soccer on Saturday. ______
4. (what) We will eat fish for dinner. ______
5. (where) They will go to the movie theater tonight. ______
6. (when) Her party will be next weekend. ______
7. (why) He will go because he likes baseball. ______
8. (how) She will go to school by bus. ______

B. Make a complete **wh-** question with **will.** Use the words in parentheses.

Example: (mall / who / see) Who will you see at the mall?

1. (open / it / how) ______
2. (when / ready / dinner) ______
3. (do / your parents / what) ______
4. (what / college / attend / your brother) ______

Name ______________________ Date ______________

Word Study

Use with student book page 426.

Vowel: u as /yu/

unicorn	**music**	**United States**
utensils	**mule**	**cube**

Say the word for each picture. First, write the word next to it. Then, circle the word that has the same vowel sound.

Example:  unicorn 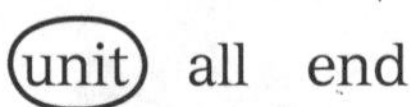 unit all end

1. ______________ fuse fit fame

2.  ______________ insect usual under

3.  ______________ open uniform exit

4.  ______________ grow cube ruler

5.  ______________ toast twelve cute

Name ______________________________ Date ____________________

Word Study

Use with student book pages 427–428.

The /oo/ Sound
Words with Multiple Meanings

A. Look at each picture. Write **oo, ue, u, ew,** or **ui** to spell the word correctly.

Example:  m __oo__ n

1.  st ____ dent

2.  j ____ ce

3. 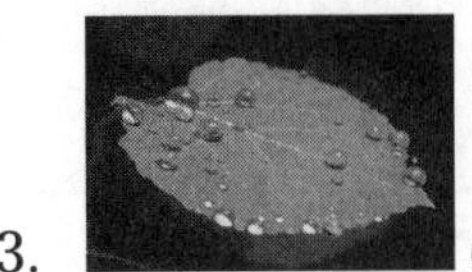  d ____

4. 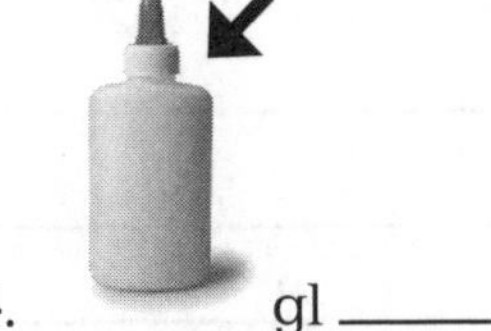 gl ____

B. Read each sentence. Circle each word with the /oo/ sound in it.

Example: The water in the (pool) feels (cool) in (July).

1. The balloon got loose and flew over the school.
2. We need glue to fix the broken stool.
3. Juice and prunes are healthy foods for you to eat.

C. Read each sentence. Circle the correct meaning or part of speech for the underlined word.

Example: I use my favorite <u>bat</u> when I play baseball.
a. an animal (b.) a tool for playing baseball

1. You can <u>fly</u> in a plane from the United States to Japan.
   a. a verb b. an insect

2. Bring the <u>can</u> of beans on our camping trip.
   a. a modal verb b. a container

3. My friend knows how to <u>play</u> the piano and the violin.
   a. a drama with actors b. a verb

Name ______________________ Date ______________

Writing Assignment

Use with student book page 429.

A Personal Narrative

Prepare to write a personal narrative about what you will do this weekend. Make a list of what you will do each day. Take notes.

Example:
- walk home from school
- eat a snack

Friday after School

- ______________________
- ______________________
- ______________________

Saturday

- ______________________
- ______________________
- ______________________
- ______________________

Sunday

- ______________________
- ______________________
- ______________________
- ______________________

Name ______________________________ Date ________________

Vocabulary From the Reading

Use with student book page 431.

Key Vocabulary
expert
fitness
healthy
physical
weight

A. Match the Key Vocabulary word with its definition.

Example: __e__ expert

1. ____ fitness
2. ____ healthy
3. ____ physical
4. ____ weight

a. how heavy something is
b. good physical health
c. connected with the body
d. state of being well; not sick
e. ~~a person who knows a lot about a topic~~

B. Fill in the blanks with the correct Key Vocabulary word.

Example: For gym teachers, ____fitness____ is a big part of their job.

1. Running is one kind of ______________ activity.
2. A doctor is an ______________ in the human body.
3. I eat a lot of vegetables to be ______________.
4. My ______________ is 93 pounds.

C. Use the words in parentheses in sentences.

Example: (physical) Physical activity is important in everyday life.

1. (fitness) ______________________________
2. (expert) ______________________________
3. (healthy) ______________________________
4. (weight) ______________________________

Name ______________________ Date ______________

Reading Strategy

Recognize Fact and Opinion

Use with student book page 432.

As you read, look for **facts** or **opinions.** Facts are true for everyone. Opinions can be different from person to person.

Academic Vocabulary for the Reading Strategy		
Word	**Explanation**	**Sample Sentence**
fact *noun*	something that is true	It is a **fact** that it rained 30 inches here last month.
opinion *noun*	a belief or idea	In my **opinion,** my team is the best baseball team.

A. Identify facts and opinions. Write **fact** or **opinion.**

Example: ____fact____ The car is red.

1. ______________ That was a great movie.
2. ______________ This pen is more expensive than that pen.
3. ______________ The dog is asleep on the carpet.
4. ______________ The dog is very friendly.
5. ______________ We are great students.
6. ______________ We are students.

B. Underline the facts and put parentheses around the opinions.

Example: There are six people in the Perry family. (All of them are friendly.)

Jean, James, Paulette, Pam, Karen, and Kristy all live in Montana. They live in a house near a stream. Jean and James are loving parents. Paulette, Pam, Karen, and Kristy are their daughters. Paulette is the tallest, and Karen is the shortest. Pam likes sports. Kristy is funny. They are a happy family.

Name ______________________________ Date ______________

Text Genre
Persuasive Text

Use with student book page 432.

A persuasive text tries to get the audience to do something.

Persuasive Text	
author's opinion	what the author believes or thinks is the right thing to do
facts	data or information to support the author's **opinion**
instructions	tell the audience what to do based on the **facts** given

Read this movie review.

The Greatest Love Story

The new movie *The Greatest Love Story* opened in theaters this weekend. This movie was the worst movie I ever saw. The plot was bad. The characters were boring. The dialogue was weak. The only good thing was the clothes. The title should be *The Greatest Clothing Story* instead of *The Greatest Love Story*. If you like pretty clothing, watch this movie. If you like good stories, stay home and read a book.

Example: What does the author say is a better title for the movie?

The Greatest Clothing Story

1. What is one fact about this movie?

____

____

2. What is one of the author's opinions about this movie?

____

____

3. What are the author's instructions if you like a good story?

____

____

4. Does the author persuade you? Do you want to see the movie?

____

____

____

Name ______________________ Date ______________

Reading Comprehension

Use with student book page 436.

A. Write the letter for the correct answer.

Example: __a__ Where was this article printed?

a. in a newspaper b. in a magazine c. on a radio station

1. ____ What did the experts say about physical activity for children and teens?

   a. It is good. b. It is bad. c. It is OK.

2. ____ How much exercise did the experts say children and teens need every day?

   a. 60 minutes b. 30 minutes c. 90 minutes

3. ____ How many hours of screen time do experts say is too much?

   a. 0 hours b. 1 hour c. 3 hours

4. ____ What kind of food is the healthiest?

   a. meat b. junk food c. vegetables

B. Answer the questions.

Example: Where was this article printed?

in a newspaper called The Daily News

1. Name three instructions the experts give to get healthier.

   ____

   ____

   ____

2. Do you think other countries have this same problem? Explain.

   ____

   ____

   ____

   ____

   ____

Name ______________________ Date ______________

Literary Element

Key Words

Use with student book page 437.

Key words are important words. They tell you the main ideas of the text. These words are usually repeated.

Identify the key words. Then circle the key words in each paragraph.

Example: The moon circles the earth every 28 days. The moon is a powerful force. It makes waves in the ocean. The moon also gives light during the night. Some people also think the moon changes how people behave.

What is the key word in the paragraph above? moon

1. Kwanzaa is a cultural celebration. African Americans celebrate Kwanzaa. This celebration lasts from December 26 to January 1. Family and unity are some of the ideas of Kwanzaa.

   What is the key word in the paragraph above? ______________

2. People who teach in a university are part of a faculty. To become part of a faculty, you must be an expert at something. Faculty members are teachers. They also write books and do research.

   What is the key word in the paragraph above? ______________

3. Someone without a place to live is called homeless. Being homeless is a problem for many people. There are many reasons someone could be homeless. One person or a whole family can be homeless.

   What is the key word in the paragraph above? ______________

4. There are many kinds of music. Sometimes music is happy. Sometimes music is sad. Sometimes music is loud. Sometimes music is soft. There are also many styles of music. Some examples are hip-hop, classical, pop, and jazz.

   What is the key word in the sentences above? ______________

5. Mushrooms are a kind of fungus. A few types are button mushrooms, shiitake mushrooms, and portabella mushrooms. Mushrooms are high in protein. They are very healthy.

   What is the key word in the paragraph above? ______________

Name ______________________ Date ______________

Writing Conventions

Use with student book page 437.

Capitalization and Punctuation: Titles

Capitalize the first word and all important words in a title. For **article** titles, use quotation marks before and after the title. For **book, magazine,** or **newspaper** titles, underline the title if you are writing it by hand, and italicize it if you are using a computer.

A. Circle **correct** if the capitalization and punctuation are correct. Circle **incorrect** if they are not correct.

Example: (newspaper) *The Daily news* (correct) incorrect

1. (book) *Grammar Sense* correct incorrect
2. (article) "Teaching English Pronunciation" correct incorrect
3. (magazine) "Time" correct incorrect
4. (newspaper) The boston globe correct incorrect
5. (article) "Surfing the Internet More Effectively" correct incorrect
6. (book) "The Painted Bird" correct incorrect

B. Handwrite these titles. Use correct capitalization and punctuation.

Example: (newspaper) The Daily news

1. (article) the recycling crisis ______________________
2. (magazine) home and garden ______________________
3. (book) webster's dictionary ______________________
4. (book) little house on the prairie ______________________
5. (newspaper) the new york times ______________________
6. (article) the high cost of space travel ______________________

Name ______________________ Date ______________

Vocabulary

Money

Use with student book pages 442–443.

ATM/debit card	credit card	gift card	quarter
cash	dollar bills	nickel	
coins	dime	penny	

A. Match the vocabulary with its meaning or example.

Example: b cash

1. ____ gift card
2. ____ quarter
3. ____ dollar bill
4. ____ price tag
5. ____ dime
6. ____ credit card

a. 25 cents
b. ~~bills or coins~~
c. a card to use only at one store
d. 10 cents
e. a card to use at any store
f. one dollar
g. tells the regular price

B. Fill in the blanks. Use the words given.

~~dollar bills~~	bargain	price tag	regular	on sale	receipt

Example: I have dollar bills in my pocket.

1. A: Why does this shirt cost less than the ______________ price?
   B: It's the sale price.

2. A: Why is this sweater half-off?
   B: It's ______________.

3. The ______________ gives the regular price.

4. This dress is half off. That's a ______________!

5. The cashier gave me change and a ______________.

Name ______________________ Date ______________

Vocabulary

Talking About Buying Things

Use with student book pages 444–445.

A. Change these numerical prices into words.

Example: $12.74 Twelve dollars and seventy-four cents.

1. $17.99 ______________________
2. $20.02 ______________________
3. $77.00 ______________________
4. $101.01 ______________________

B. Unscramble the letters in parentheses. Then write the words in the blanks.

Rose: Do you have any **(example)** coins (sinco)

Anna: Yes, I have two (1) ____________ (sterrqua), three (2) ____________ (smedi), a (3) ____________ (kelnic) and four (4) ____________ (snienep).

Rose: How much (5) ____________ (yemon) is that?

Anna: That's 89 (6) ____________ (stenc).

C. Complete the conversation. Fill in the blanks with the correct vocabulary words. Use the list below.

~~cost~~	credit cards	receipt	sale	half	price

Quan: How much does this belt **(example)** cost?

Salesclerk: The (1) ____________ is $10.

Julia: Is it on (2) ____________?

Salesclerk: Yes, it's (3) ____________ off.

Quan: Do you take (4) ____________?

Salesclerk: Yes, thank you. Here is your (5) ____________.

Name ______________________ Date ______________

Grammar

Use with student book page 446.

Future with going to

Tran **will pay** with cash.	→	Tran **is going to pay** with cash.
Olga **will buy** a sweater.	→	Olga **is going to buy** a sweater.
Martin **will use** a coupon.	→	Martin **is going to use** a coupon.

I am going to buy a book.	**We are** going to buy a book.
You are going to buy a book.	**You are** going to buy a book.
He / She / It is going to buy a book.	**They are** going to buy a book.

A. Fill in the blanks with the correct verb form. Use **be going to** with the verbs in parentheses.

Example: He is going to buy a book from the bookstore. (buy)

1. The students ______________ a test on Tuesday. (take)
2. We ______________ to Hawaii during summer vacation. (go)
3. My Aunt Lauren ______________ French. (study)
4. I ______________ to bed in a few hours. (go)

B. Circle **correct** if the sentences are correct and **incorrect** if they are not correct.

Example: He going to buying books at the bookstore. **correct** **(incorrect)**

1. My Spanish class is going to go to Mexico for a week. **correct** **incorrect**
2. He is going to drive them to the mall. **correct** **incorrect**
3. We going wear yellow pants to the pep rally. **correct** **incorrect**
4. They is going to sleep at their grandmother's tonight. **correct** **incorrect**

C. Pretend you have one million dollars. What are you going to do? Write three sentences. Use the correct form of **be going to.**

Example: I am going to buy a new house for my family.

1. ______________________________
2. ______________________________
3. ______________________________

Name ______________________ Date ______________

D. Correct the mistakes.

Example: Am going to buying a new house for my family. I am going to buy a new house for my family.

1. He going drive to work now. ______________
2. We are going go camping. ______________
3. Am go to shop at the mall. ______________
4. They are going to sailing across the English Channel. ______________
5. She are going to buy what is on sale. ______________
6. My sister and I going to see a movie tonight. ______________
7. Our teachers going to meet with our parents next week. ______________
8. Luis's grandparents go to visit him next summer. ______________
9. All of the students is go to visit the natural history museum next week. ______________

Homophones are words that sound the same when you say them, but they are spelled differently and mean different things.

E. Write the correct homophone.

Example: I am going to buy some milk.	**by**	**buy**	**bye**
1. I am going to walk ________ the store.	**by**	**buy**	**bye**
2. My uncle is going to buy a new ________ for his boat.	**sale**		**sail**
3. The baby is going to say "________" when we leave.	**by**	**buy**	**bye**
4. He is going to ________ a new jacket.	**by**	**buy**	**bye**
5. I am going to buy the shoes that are on ________.	**sale**		**sail**

Name ______________________ Date ______________

Grammar Expansion

Will and going to

You can use **will** and **going to** + verb to explain or predict future events. Use **will** to make a promise or a request. Use **going to** to talk about a plan or an intention.

will / going to	Meaning	Example
will	promise	I **will** pick you up after school today.
	request	**Will** you buy some milk at the store?
going to	plan	I am **going to** go camping this weekend.
	intention	He is **going to** do his homework now.

A. Read the sentences. Circle the meaning of **will** or **going to**.

Example: He is **going to** travel to Ecuador next month. **(plan)** **promise**

1. I **will** finish my homework before dinner. **promise** **request**
2. **Will** you wake up your grandmother? **promise** **request**
3. They are **going to** go on a field trip next week. **plan** **request**
4. We are **going to** study together now. **request** **intention**

B. Read the sentences. Write the meaning of **will** or **going to.**

Example: ____plan____ He is going to get married in two months.

1. ______________ We are going to go to a concert after dinner.
2. ______________ Will you go to the bank for me?
3. ______________ I am going to do my homework.
4. ______________ I will help you.

C. Now make sentences using **will** and **going to.** Use the meanings in parentheses.

Example: (plan) He is going to get married in two months.

1. (promise) ______________________
2. (request) ______________________
3. (plan) ______________________
4. (intention) ______________________

Name ______________________________ Date ____________________

Word Study

Use with student book page 448.

The /aw/ Sound

A. Look at each picture. Circle the correct spelling for the name of the picture.

Example: pall (paw) pau

1. tall tawl taul
5. allthor awthor author
2. hall hawl haul
6. lalln lawn laun
3. sall saw sau
7. sidewalk sidewallk sidewaulk
4. ball bawl baul
8. alltomobile awtomobile automobile

B. Write a word to finish each sentence.

Example: Let's go to the bookstore at the ___mall___.

1. The big truck can ______________ a lot of gear.
2. I have read all of the books by my favorite ______________.
3. You should walk on the ______________, not in the street.
4. The grass is too long, so I will mow the ______________.
5. My dog knows how to give me her ______________.
6. Let's go outside and play catch with the ______________.

Name ______________________________ Date ______________

Writing Assignment

Descriptive Paragraph

Use with student book page 449.

Prepare to write a descriptive paragraph about five of your classmates. What do you think they will buy when they go shopping? Think about what they like to do to help you guess.

A. Write a list of five people. Take notes on their interests.

Names	Interests	
Example: Josh	loves movies	plays basketball
1.		
2.		
3.		
4.		
5.		

B. Now make one sentence about each classmate with **will** or **going to.** Use your notes.

Example: Josh will buy some DVDs because he loves movies.

1. ______________________________

2. ______________________________

3. ______________________________

4. ______________________________

5. ______________________________

Name ______________________ Date ______________

Vocabulary From the Reading

Use with student book page 451.

Key Vocabulary
budget
discount
expenses
percent
value

A. Match the Key Vocabulary word and its definition.

Example: __e__ budget

1. ____ discount
2. ____ expenses
3. ____ percent
4. ____ value

a. a lowered price
b. a number out of 100
c. how much something costs
d. how much money you regularly pay
~~e. a plan of how much money you can spend~~

B. Use the correct Key Vocabulary word to complete the sentences.

Example: My parents have a monthly ____budget____ for their expenses.

1. My parents have many ______________ such as food and gas.
2. Students get a ______________ at the bookstore.
3. This shirt has a 10 ______________ discount.
4. The ______________ of this phone is $100.

C. Now make sentences with the Key Vocabulary words in parentheses.

Example: (expenses) Cars and groceries are examples of expenses.

1. (percent) ______________________________
2. (discount) ______________________________
3. (budget) ______________________________
4. (value) ______________________________

Name ________________________ Date ________________

Reading Strategy

Use with student book page 452.

Make and Confirm Predictions

A prediction is something you guess will happen. If you find your guess is correct, you confirm the prediction. As you read, make predictions about what comes next.

Academic Vocabulary for the Reading Strategy		
Word	**Explanation**	**Sample Sentence**
confirm	prove that something is true	Researchers studied teen shoppers to **confirm** that those who learned money math were smarter shoppers.
prediction	a guess about what will happen in the future	Many educators have made the **prediction** that teens who learn money math will become smarter shoppers.

Identify the predictions and the confirmations. Write **prediction** or **confirmation.**

Example: confirmation An experiment proved this to be true.

1. ________________ Scientists show that animals can learn to use tools.
2. ________________ It will snow tomorrow.
3. ________________ My father will be home before 6:00 tonight.
4. ________________ My father came home before 6:00 last night.
5. ________________ I saw the dish fall. The dish is broken.
6. ________________ I think we will have a quiz tomorrow.
7. ________________ The map shows where the war happened.
8. ________________ He will make a lot of money.
9. ________________ My teacher said this answer is correct.
10. ________________ I read that in the dictionary.
11. ________________ He will do well on his test.
12. ________________ I saw this movie before.

Name ______________________ Date ______________

Text Genre

Use with student book page 452.

Informational Text: Web Article

Informational texts give information. Web articles have many features to help explain information.

Informational Text	
headings	what each section is about
facts	true information
predictions	things the Web site tells you will happen if you follow instructions
instructions	statements that tell you what to do

Read the Web article.

The Dangers of Credit Cards

General Information

Most Americans have at least four credit cards. Some even have 50 credit cards. Do you know people who use credit cards? People who have credit cards should learn more about how they work.

Interest Rates

If you have a credit card, the interest rate is the percentage of money you pay to use your credit card. An example of an interest rate is 20 percent. That means if you use your credit card to spend $100 at a store, you also pay 20 percent more. $100 plus 20 percent is $120.

Suggestions

Credit cards can be dangerous. Don't use them often or you will owe too much money. If you don't owe money, you won't have a problem with interest or late fees.

Now answer the questions.

Example: What is the title of this text? The Dangers of Credit Cards

1. What are the three headings in this article? ______________________

____

2. Write two facts from this article. ______________________

____

3. Give an example of instructions in the article. ______________________

____

4. What prediction does the article make? ______________________

____

Name ______________________________ Date ______________

Reading Comprehension

Use with student book page 458.

A. Write the letter of the correct answer.

Example: b What are two examples of coins?

a. $1 and $5 b. quarter and nickel c. 75 cents

1. What instructions does the author give to help with money problems?
   a. Talk to adults.
   b. Take a class about money.
   c. Learn money math now.

2. What will understanding percentage help you know?
   a. regular price b. sale price c. a grid

3. If 53 percent of 100 teens say they like shopping at the mall, how many teens say they like shopping at the mall?
   a. 100 teens b. 53 teens c. 47 teens

4. How do you calculate a discount?
   a. Sale Price − Discount = Regular Price
   b. Regular Price − Discount = Sale Price

B. Answer the questions.

1. Give two examples of fixed expenses.
   - ______________________________
   - ______________________________

2. Give two examples of flexible expenses.
   - ______________________________
   - ______________________________

3. Explain in your own words why a budget is important.

____

____

____

Name ______________________ Date ______________

Text Elements

Use with student book page 459.

Using Headings and Signpost Words to Make Predictions

Predictions are when you guess what might happen. **Headings** help you predict the content of the text. **Signpost words** also help you make predictions. Signpost words tell you something different is coming or hint at what happens next.

A. You are going to read a section of an article called "Thinking About Buying: A Warning." Make a prediction. What do you think it will be about?

____

____

B. Now read the passage.

Thinking About Buying: A Warning

People today spend too much money. For example, we buy expensive things at malls. As a result, we spend too much money. We often buy things we don't need. Now, what can we do? At first, we should think about the things we buy. We should ask ourselves, "Can we use that money in a better way?"

1. List the four signpost words you found in the paragraph.

______________ ______________

______________ ______________

2. Now choose one signpost word. Tell what prediction it helped you make.

____

____

____

3. Choose another signpost word. Tell what prediction it helped you make.

____

____

____

Name ______________________ Date ______________

Writing Numerals

Write the numbers.

1 1

2 2

3 3

4 4

5 5

6 6

7 7

8 8

9 9

10 10

Name ______________________________ Date ________________

Writing Numerals

Write the numbers.

11 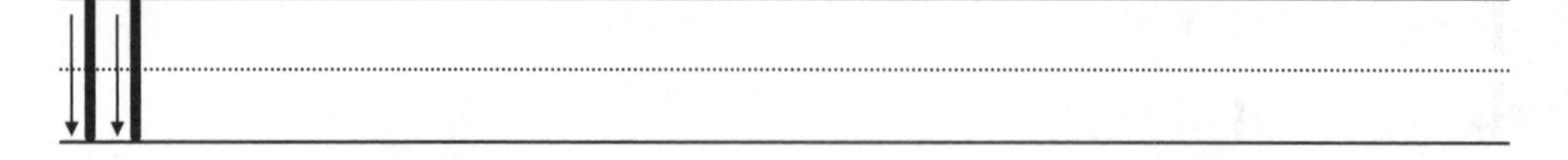

12 

13 

14 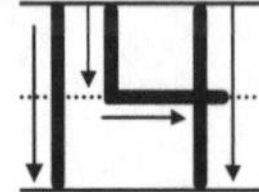

15 

16 

17 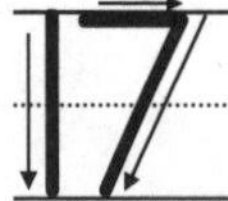

18 

19 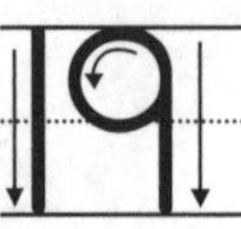

20 20

Name ______________________ Date ______________

Writing Numerals

Write the numbers.

10 10

20 20

30 30

40 40

50 50

60 60

70 70

80 80

90 90

100 100

Name ______________________________ Date ________________

Writing Cursive

Write the capital and lowercase letters in cursive.

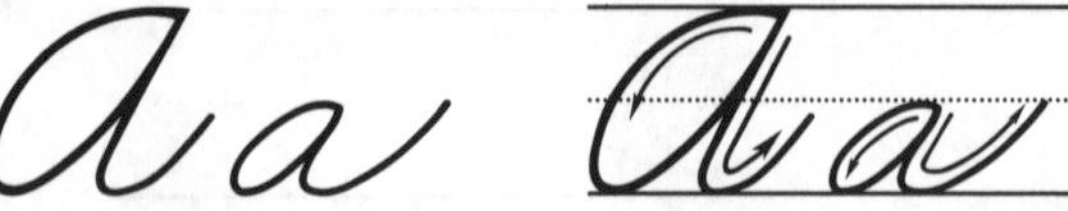

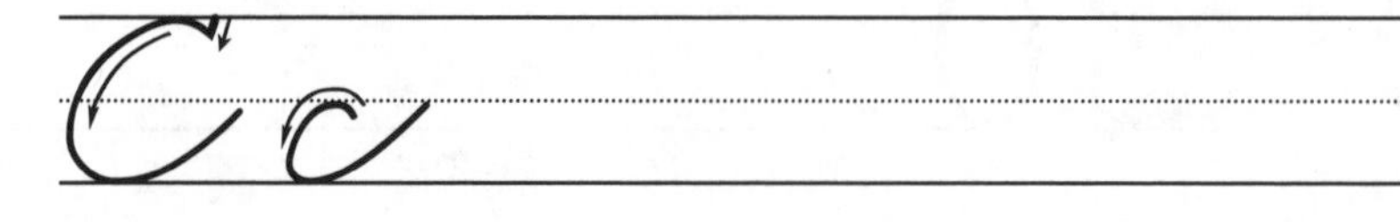

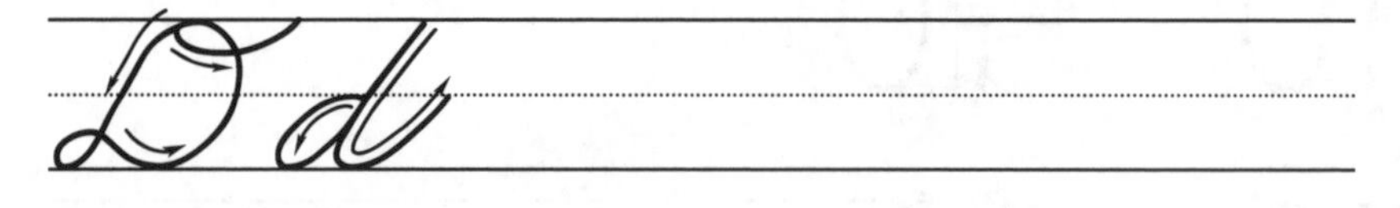

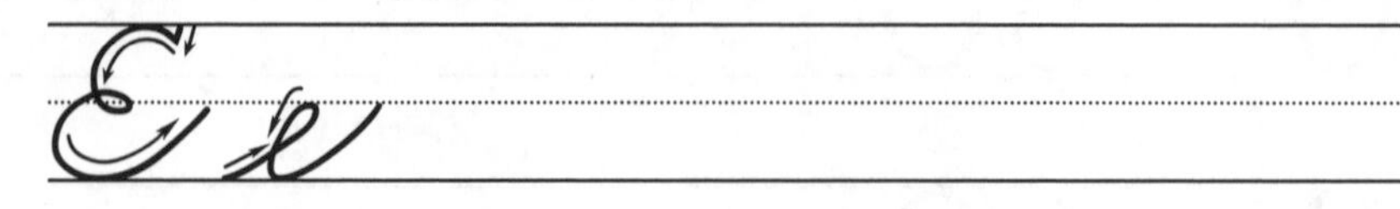

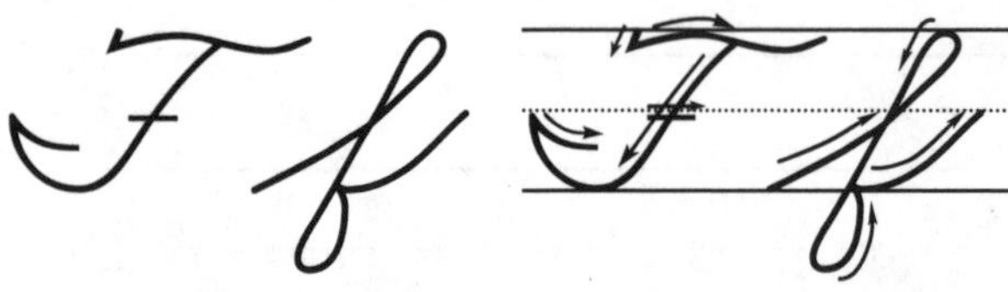

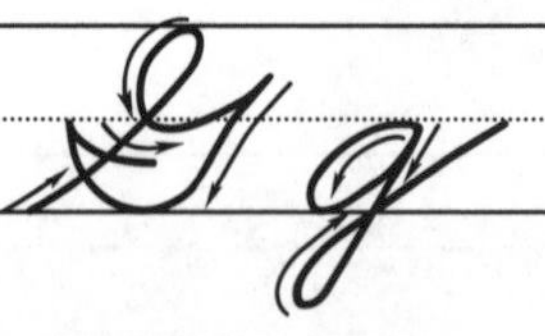

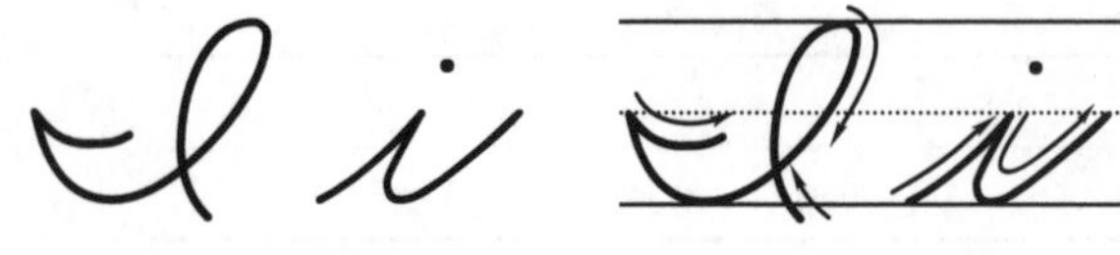

Name ______________________ Date ______________

Writing Cursive

Write the capital and lowercase letters in cursive.

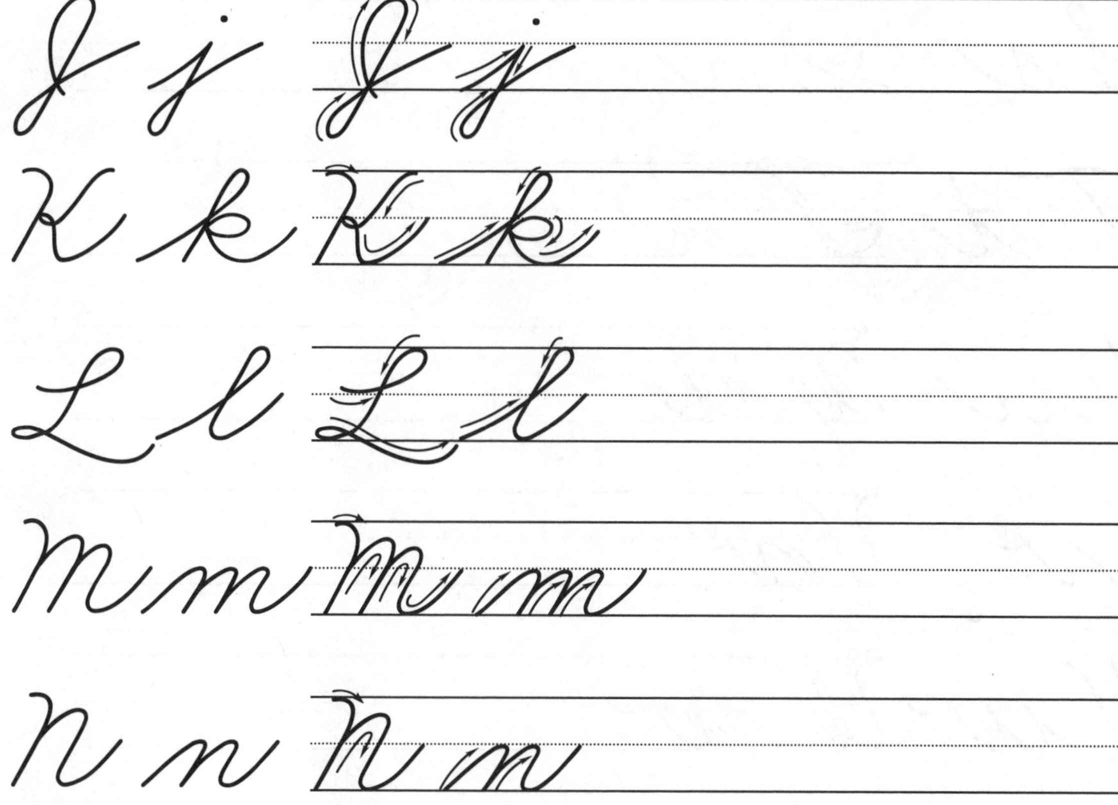

Name ______________________ Date ______________

Writing Cursive

Write the capital and lowercase letters in cursive.

Ss Ss

Tt Tt

Uu Uu

Vv Vv

Ww Ww

Xx Xx

Yy Yy

Zz Zz

Circle the matching letters.

1. 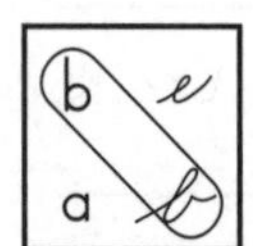

2. 

3. 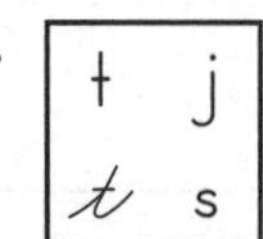

4. 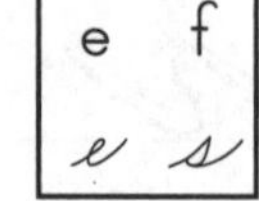

5. 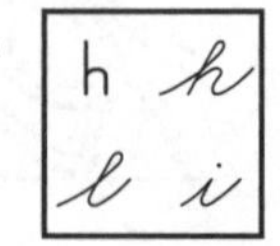

6. r n
r p